A TREASURY OF

WALL STREET

WISDOM

Edited By

HARRY D. SCHULTZ

&

SAMSON COSLOW

INVESTORS' PRESS, INC. • PALISADES PARK, NEW JERSEY

Library of Congress Catalog Card Number 67-2478

Published by Investors' Press, Inc.
Palisades Park, New Jersey 07650

MANUFACTURED IN THE UNITED STATES OF AMERICA
BY DURANE PRINTING COMPANY, INC., NEW YORK, NEW YORK 10010

"IF I WANTED TO BECOME A TRAMP I WOULD SEEK INFORMATION AND ADVICE FROM THE MOST SUC-CESSFUL TRAMP I COULD FIND. IF I WANTED TO BECOME A FAILURE I WOULD SEEK ADVICE FROM MEN WHO HAD NEVER SUCCEEDED. IF I WANTED TO SUCCEED IN ALL THINGS, I WOULD LOOK AROUND ME FOR THOSE WHO ARE SUCCEEDING AND DO AS THEY HAVE DONE."

JOSEPH MARSHALL WADE

TABLE OF CONTENTS

PART I

Introduction

You have in your hands the refined and filtered nectar from some of the keenest minds who have ever played an important role in Wall Street since its inception.

To bring you this Anthology of Wall Street Wisdom we have searched the libraries and private book collections; scanned microfilm, contacted living relatives of some of the Greats, and generally unearthed and uprooted everything and everybody who could be helpful in our all-out effort.

Books about investing are great in number, but few are wholly satisfactory. Still, it is seldom possible to skim through the most uneven of stock market manuals without emerging with at least one or two workable ideas. It was this paradox that led to the anthology of writings on investment philosophy presented here. In each case, the fat was carefully pared away, and the meat of the argument was left. Recognizing that one man's meat is another man's poison, a great variety of techniques and methods is included, from the earliest days on Wall Street to the present day.

At one stage or another in the career of almost every stock market trader, he devours stock market "methods" books—all sorts and sizes, from the classic writings of Dow to the most obscure "sure-fire" trading technique of some anonymous operator of the Twenties. From this reading program, the inquisitive investor will often discover refinements that can greatly improve his own methods.

Successful buying and selling of stocks is usually a lonely business. Behind consistent success, there usually lies a plan. And a plan able to sustain a profitable trading program is usually the result of a step-by-step thinking through of the sequences and signals that can guide the day-to-day execution. The working out of such a systematic program is often assisted by placing it alongside the detailed methods of other successful traders and critically evaluating each stage.

The selections which follow are presented, more or less, in chronological order. Over the years, the rules change and the types of actual operations are radically overhauled to match the new conditions in each era. But the objectives and motivations of the great Wall Street writers remain remarkably constant. It is the insights into these changeless aspects of market trading that are anthologized. In our final compilation, we endeavored to select the **essence**—the most important things and thoughts that these brilliant financial minds have recorded for posterity.

As Wall Street began to develop its characteristic methods around the time of the Civil War, trading was dominated by the Great Operators. These operators sought to carve out transportation empires and used the stock market as one of their critical battlefields. There are still some who go to Wall Street today seeking empires— such as the raiders shopping among the corporate shells and the closely held companies with relatively few shares outstanding.

Of more interest to the present day investor or trader are the efforts of the earlier stock market operators to follow the ebb and flow of market values through "readings" or signals taken periodically. The nature of these signals varies widely. One trader favors buying "undervalued" stocks or those with high yields, while another would buy only those stocks moving up on volume or forming a particularly "favorable" chart pattern. It was the development of these "methods" by Charles Dow and the other pioneers that established the necessary groundwork for the Cult of Common Stocks, as it first fully blossomed in the Twenties and has continued to flow right up to the present.

Without these guide lines, that at least on paper held out some promise of ultimate success, it is doubtful whether many small investors would have ventured so boldly into Wall Street. Therefore, it might be said that the leading approaches to investing that have stirred the public and motivated their purchases are introduced in this anthology. Each of these methods is presented in the exact words of the person who gave it its most eloquent and convincing expression. Together, they provide a review of the basic wisdom of Wall Street as it has appeared to several generations of market observers. It is hoped that this storehouse will add to the wisdom of Wall Street operators of today, and of those yet to come.

Part I

The Dow Theorists . . .

CHARLES H. DOW . . The Grandfather of Technical Analysis.

SAMUEL A. NELSON . . Author and Dow Theory Compiler.

WILLIAM P. HAMILTON . . Pioneer Technician and Successor to Dow.

ROBERT RHEA . . Dow Historian and Record Keeper.

RICHARD RUSSELL . . Leading Present-Day Dow Theorist.

CHARLES H. DOW

A cornerstone name . . .

The Grandfather of Technical Analysis

One of the most frequently spoken words on Wall Street **any** day is DOW. "How is the Dow today?" is the commonest question put to brokers. The man who contributed his name to this (Dow-Jones Average) and to the equally famous "Dow Theory" was Charles H. Dow, who was born in Sterling, Connecticut on November 6, 1851.

Records of the New York Stock Exchange indicate that Dow was a partner of Goodbody, Glynn and Dow from December 1885 to April 1891. This, however, was a technicality. Dow became a partner merely because Robert Goodbody was not yet a naturalized citizen, and Dow held the seat only until Goodbody's citizenship came through. Even so, Dow executed orders on the floor and held the seat for several years, which was long enough to get an insider's view and feel of the market. (Goodbody & Company is still a major Wall Street house.)

But Dow was primarily a newspaper man, earning his income from this calling all of his working life. Starting on several New England newspapers, in 1880 he came to New York City as a financial reporter, writing articles and editorials for the *New York Mail* and *Express*. Thereafter he joined the Kiernan News Agency, where he met Edward D. Jones, a fellow worker. The two soon left Kiernan to form their own firm—Dow, Jones and Company—

which started by delivering "flimsies" or "slips" to financial institutions of Wall Street. July 8, 1889 saw the first edition of *The Wall Street Journal* with Dow as editor and founder.

Dow's editorials were written as just that, and not as a series of articles putting forth a specific theory. Since these editorials accurately reflected Dow's remarkably analytical thinking, S. A. Nelson put them together and called them, in toto, ".Dow's Theory," of which Nelson became the first disciple.

Dow was modest in dress, in speech and in manner. He was a typical New Englander, intelligent, self-repressed, ultra-conservative, and he knew his business. He was said to be almost judicially cold in the consideration of any subject, whatever the fervor of discussion. His co-worker, William Hamilton, said of him, "It would be less than just to say that I never saw him angry, I never saw him even excited. His perfect integrity and good sense commanded the confidence of every man in Wall Street, at a time when there were few efficient newspaper men covering the financial section, and of these fewer with any depth of knowledge of finance."

An early associate on the Journal, Thomas F. Woodlock, said, "Dow was a tall, black-bearded, slightly stooping man, with a grave air and the measured speech of a college professor."

Hamilton once gave a fair and balanced appraisal of Dow's approach to the market:

"Knowing and liking Dow, with whom I worked in the last years of his life, I was often, with many of his friends, exasperated by his over-conservatism. It showed itself particularly in his editorials in *The Wall Street Journal,* to which it is now necessary to allude because they are the only written record of Dow's theory of price movement. He would write a strong, readable and convincing editorial, on a public question affecting finance and business and in the last paragraph would add safeguards and saving clauses which not merely took the sting out of it but took the 'Wallop' out of it. In the language of the prize ring he pulled his punches.

CHARLES H. DOW

"He was almost too cautious to come out with a flat, dogmatic statement of this Theory, however sound it was and however close and clear his reasoning might be. He wrote, mostly in 1901 and the first half of 1902, a number of editorials dealing with methods of stock speculation.

"But what may be commended is Dow's clarity and sterling good sense. What he had to say was worth saying and he stopped when he had said it—a rare virtue in editorial writing. His feeling for the essential fact and for the underlying truth, without which the fact is bare and impertinent, will be readily remarked. He dealt with speculation as a fact, and could still show forth its truth without profitless moralizing, or confusing it with gambling. It will be well to imitate his point of view in further discussion, both on his Theory and on the immense and useful significance of the stock market generally."

Dow died at the age of 51, in December 1902.

It is a matter of regret that Dow spoke to the world solely through his few editorials written within a three-year period early in the century for *The Wall Street Journal.* Poring through this scant supply of word-age now, one wonders whether perhaps the entire Dow legend may have been magnified all out of proportion by his later followers, and whether they have read into it more than its author actually conceived. Nevertheless, there is no doubt that Dow's source material provided the germ—as microscopic as it was—for the Theory which was later amplified by others into the now familiar concepts: The three market movements that go on simultaneously (major, secondary, and minor); the "higher tops and bottoms" and "lower tops and bottoms" that constitute the cornerstone of Dow Theory signals; the confirmations of the Industrial and Rail Averages, and the other well known theorems. Dow himself would probably have been the last one to suspect that an entire forecasting philosophy would evolve from his fragmentary day-to-day market comments, yet as crude as they may sound now, they were new and original in their day. They opened up new worlds and new horizons for his successors: S. A. Nelson, the first man to recognize

5

this breakthrough in stock market thinking, and who first "organized" Dow's writings in book form in 1903; Hamilton, Dow's successor as editor of *The Wall Street Journal,* an astute understudy who continued the tradition and who possibly contributed more to Dow Theory as it is known today than Dow himself; Rhea, who took Dow and Hamilton's basic principles and formulated them into an actual "system"; and Russell, who clarified much of the Theory's ambiguities and integrated them with the market concepts of today.

A few well-remembered examples of Charles Dow's writings of the early 1900's follows.

The Wisdom of
CHARLES H. DOW

Three General Lines of Reasoning...

WE HAVE SPOKEN in a preceding article of the fact that the experience of great interests in the market seems to have crystallized into three general lines of reasoning.

The first is that the surface appearance of the market is apt to be deceptive. The second is that it is well in trading to cut losses short and let profits run. The third is that correctly discounting the future is a sure and easy road to wealth. The problem is how these rules, which are undoubtedly sound, can be operated in a practical way.

Let us take first the action of the general market with reference to the time to buy. The market is always to be considered as having three movements, all going on at the same time. The first is the narrow movement from day to day. The second is the short swing, running from two weeks to a month or more; the third is the main movement covering at least four years in its duration.

The day to day movement should be disregarded by everybody, except traders, who pay no commissions. The medium swing is the one for ordinary consideration.

8

The outside trader should not attempt to deal in more than two or three stocks at a time. He should keep a chart of the price movements of these stocks so as to know their swings for months or years, and thus be able to tell readily where in the general swing his particular stocks appear to be.

He should keep with his price movement a record of the volume of transactions and notes of any special facts bearing on that property, such as increases or decreases in earnings, increases in fixed charges, development of floating debt, and above all the actual dividend earnings as shown from month to month. He should observe the movement of the general market as indicated by the averages published daily, as this shows the market more clearly than it is shown by any one stock.

The main purpose of this study is to enable the trader to determine, first, the value of the stock he is in; whether it is increasing or decreasing and, second, when the time to buy seems opportune. Assuming the thirty day swing to be about 5 points, it is in the highest degree desirable not to buy when three of these points have passed, as such a purchase limits the probable profits to about two points.

It is therefore generally wise to look for a low point on a decline. Suppose, for instance, that Union Pacific was the stock under consideration; that it was clearly selling below its value, and that a bull market for the four-year period was under way. Assuming further that in a period of reaction Union Pacific had fallen four points from the previous highest. Assume earnings and prospects to be favorable and the outlook for the general market to be about normal.

This would be the time to begin to buy Union Pacific. The prudent trader, however, would take only part of his line. He would buy perhaps one-half of the stock he wanted and then give an order to buy the remainder as the price declined. The fall might go much further than he anticipated. It might be necessary to wait a long time for profit. There might even be developments which would make it wise to throw over the stock bought with the hope of replacing it materially lower.

9

These, however, are all exceptions. In a majority of cases this method of choosing the time to buy, founded upon clear perception of value in the stock chosen and close observation of the market swings under way will enable an operator to secure stock at a time and at a price which will give fair profits on the investment.

Swings Within Swings

A CORRESPONDENT ASKS: "For some time you have been writing rather bullish on the immediate market, yet a little bearish in a larger sense. How do you make this consistent?"

We get this question in one form or another rather frequently. It denotes a lack of familiarity with fluctuations in prices when viewed over considerable periods. Many people seem to think that the change in prices in any one day is complete in itself and bears no relation to the larger movements which may be under way. This is not so.

Nothing is more certain than that the market has three well defined movements which fit into each other. The first is the daily variation due to local causes and the balance of buying or selling at that particular time. The secondary movement covers a period ranging from ten days to sixty days, averaging probably between thirty and forty days. The third move is the great swing covering from four to six years.

In thinking about the market, it is necessary to think with reference to each of these periods in order to take advantage of opportunities. If the main move is up, relapses are speculators' opportunities, but if the main move is down, rallies furnish these opportunities.

Losses should not generally be taken on the long side in a bull period. Nor should they generally be taken on the short side in a bear period. It is a bull period as long as the average of one high point exceeds that of previous high points. It is a bear period when the low point becomes lower than the previous low points. It is often difficult to judge whether the end of an advance has come because the movement of prices is that which would occur if the main tendency had changed. Yet, it may only be a pronounced secondary movement.

The first thing for any operator to consider is the value of the stock in which he proposes to trade. The second is to determine the direction of the main movement of prices. We know of nothing more instructive on this point than the course of prices as printed daily. The third thing is to determine the position of the secondary swing.

Assume for instance that the stock selected was Union Pacific; that the course of prices afforded clear evidence of a bull market under way; that the high point in Union Pacific thirty days ago was 108; that the price had slowly declined in sympathy with the market and without special new features to 98. The chances would be in favor of buying a part of the line wanted at that price with the intention of buying a little more if the stock had further decline or if the price showed a well defined advancing tendency. It would then be wise to watch the general market and wait for an advance.

A 10-point decline under such conditions would be almost certain to bring in a bull market more than 5 points recovery and full 10 points would not be unreasonable; hence if the general market maintained a good tone, it would be wise to wait for 5 points and then begin to think about stop orders.

Even in a bear market, this method of trading will usually be found safe, although the profit taken should be less because of the liability of weak spots breaking out and checking the general rise.

Methods of Reading the Market

A CORRESPONDENT WRITES: "Is there any way of forecasting the course of the market from the tape, from your records of transactions or from the summarized movement of prices? Transactions must mean something, but how can a trader tell what they mean?"

This is an old question. There have been a variety of answers but it is doubtful if any have been or can be wholly satisfactory. Several methods, however, are in practical use and at times afford suggestions.

There is what is called the book method.* Prices are set down, giving each change of 1 point as it occurs, forming thereby lines having a general horizontal direction but running into diagonals as the market moves up and down. There come times when a stock with a good degree of activity will stay within a narrow range of prices, say 2 points, until there has formed quite a long horizontal line of these figures. The formation of such a line sometimes suggests that stock has been accumulated or distributed, and this **leads other people** to buy or sell at the same time. Records of this kind kept for the last fifteen years seem to

* One of the earliest descriptions of point-and-figure.

support the theory that the manipulation necessary to acquire stock is often times detected in this way.

Another method is what is called the theory of double tops. Records of trading show that in many cases when a stock reaches top it will have a moderate decline and then go back again to near the highest figures. If after such a move, the price again recedes, it is liable to decline some distance.

Those, however, who attempt to trade on this theory alone find many exceptions and a good many times when signals are not given.

There are those who trade on the theory of averages. It is true that in a considerable period of time the market has about as many days of advance as it has of decline. If there come a series of days of advance, there will almost surely come the balancing days of decline.

The trouble with this system is that the small swings are always part of the larger swings, and while the tendency of events equally liable to happen is always toward equality, it is also true that every combination possible is liable to occur, and there frequently come long swings, or, in the case of stock trading, an extraordinary number of days of advance or decline which fit properly into the theory when regarded on a long scale, but which are calculated to upset any operations based on the expectation of a series of short swings.

A much more practicable theory is that founded on the law of action and reaction. It seems to be a fact that a primary movement in the market will generally have a secondary movement in the opposite direction of at least three-eighths of the primary movement. If a stock advances 10 points, it is very likely to have a relapse of 4 points or more. The law seems to hold good no matter how far the advance goes. A rise of 20 points will not infrequently bring a decline of 8 points or more.

It is impossible to tell in advance the length of any primary movement, but the further it goes, the greater the reaction when it comes, hence the more certainty of being able to trade successfully on that reaction.

A method employed by some operators of large experience is that of responses. The theory involved is this: The market is always under more or less manipulation. A large operator who is seeking to advance the market does not buy everything on the list, but puts up two or three leading stocks either by legitimate buying or by manipulation. He then watches the effect on the other stocks. If sentiment is bullish, and people are disposed to take hold, those who see this rise in two or three stocks immediately begin to buy other stocks and the market rises to a higher level. This is the public response, and is an indication that the leading stocks will be given another lift and that the general market will follow.

If, however, leading stocks are advanced and others do not follow, it is evidence that the public is not disposed to buy. As soon as this is clear the attempt to advance prices is generally discontinued. This method is employed more particularly by those who watch the tape. But it can be read at the close of the day in our record of transactions by seeing what stocks were put up within specified hours and whether the general market followed or not. The best way of reading the market is to read from the standpoint of values. The market is not like a balloon plunging hither and thither in the wind. As a whole, it represents a serious, well considered effort on the part of far-sighted and well-informed men to adjust prices to such values as exist or which are expected to exist in the not too remote future. The thought with great operators is not whether a price can be advanced, but whether the value of property which they propose to buy will lead investors and speculators six months hence to take stock at figures from 10 to 20 points above present prices.

In reading the market, therefore, the main point is to discover what a stock can be expected to be worth three months hence and then to see whether manipulators or investors are advancing the price of that stock toward those figures. It is often possible to read movements in the market very clearly in this way. To know values is to comprehend the meaning of movements in the market.

The "Ten Year Cycle" Theory

A CORRESPONDENT WRITES: "Is it true that commercial or stock exchange panics are approximately periodic in their occurrence?"

The facts point distinctly in that direction, and there is reason back of the facts. The reason is that the business community has a tendency to go from one extreme to the other. As a whole, it is either contracting business under a belief that prices will be lower or expanding under a belief that prices will be higher. It appears to take ordinarily five or six years for public confidence to go from the point of too little hope to the point of too much confidence and then five or six years more to get back to the condition of hopelessness.

This ten-year movement in England is given in detail by Professor Jevons in his attempt to show that sun spots have some bearing upon commercial affairs. Without going into the matter of sun spots and their bearing upon crops, commerce, or states of minds, it may be assumed that Professor Jevons has stated correctly the periods of depression as they have occurred in England during the last two centuries.

The dates given by him as the years in which commercial crises have occurred follow: 1701, 1711, 1712, 1731-2, 1742, 1752, 1763, 1772-3, 1783, 1793, 1804-5, 1815, 1825, 1836, 1847, 1857, 1866 and 1878.

This makes a very good showing for the ten-year theory, and it is supported to a considerable extent by what has occurred in this country during the past century.

The first crisis in the United States during the nineteenth century came in 1814, and was precipitated by the capture of Washington by the British on the 24th of August in that year. The Philadelphia and New York banks suspended payments, and for a time the crisis was acute. The difficulties leading up to this period were the great falling off in foreign trade caused by the embargo and non-intercourse acts of 1808, the excess of public expenditures over public receipts, and the creation of a large number of state banks taking the place of the old United States bank. Many of these state banks lacked capital and issued currency without sufficient security.

There was a near approach to a crisis in 1819 as the result of a tremendous contraction of bank circulation. The previous increases of bank issues had promoted speculation, the contraction caused a serious fall in the prices of commodities and real estate. This, however, was purely a money panic as far as its causes were concerned.

The European crisis in 1825 caused a diminished demand for American products and led to lower prices and some money stringency in 1826. The situation, however, did not become very serious and was more in the nature of an interruption to progress than a reversal of conditions.

The year 1837 brought a great commercial panic, for which there was abundant cause. There had been rapid industrial and commercial growth, with a multitude of enterprises established ahead of the time. Crops were deficient, and breadstuffs were imported. The refusal of the government to extend the charter of the United States Bank had caused a radical change in the banking business of the country, while the withdrawal of public deposits and their lodgment with state banks had given the foundation for abnormal speculation.

The panic in Europe in 1847 exerted but little influence in this country, although there was a serious loss in specie, and the Mexican war had some effect in checking enterprises. These effects, however, were neutralized somewhat by large exports of breadstuffs and later by the discovery of gold in 1848-9.

There was a panic of the first magnitude in 1857, following the failure of the Ohio Life Insurance & Trust Company in August. This panic came unexpectedly, although prices had been falling for some months. There had been very large railroad building, and the proportion of specie held by banks was very small in proportion to their loans and deposits. One of the features of this period was the great number of failures. The banks generally suspended payments in October.

The London panic in 1866 precipitated by the failure of Overend, Guerney & Co., was followed by heavy fall in prices in the Stock Exchange here. In April there had been a corner in Michigan Southern and rampant speculation generally, from which the relapse was rather more than normal.

The panic of September, 1873, was a commercial as well as a Stock Exchange panic. It was the outcome of an enormous conversion of floating into fixed capital. Business had been expanded on an enormous scale, and the supply of money became insufficient for the demands made upon it. Credit collapsed and the depression was extremely serious.

The year 1884 brought a Stock Exchange smash but not a commercial crisis. The failure of the Marine Bank, Metropolitan Bank and Grant & Ward in May was accompanied by a large fall in prices and a general check which was felt throughout the year. The Trunk Line war, which had lasted for several years, was one of the factors in this period.

The panic of 1893 was the outcome of a number of causes—uncertainty in regard to the currency situation, the withdrawal of foreign investments and the fear of radical tariff legislation. The anxiety in regard to the maintenance of the gold standard was undoubtedly the chief factor, as it bore upon many others.

Judging by the past and by the developments of the last six years, it is not unreasonable to suppose that we may get at least a stock exchange flurry in the next few years. This decade seems to be the one for the small crisis instead of the large one—a type of 1884 rather than a recurrence of 1837, 1873 or 1893.

Cutting Losses Short

WE HAVE SPOKEN in previous articles of methods of trading. Experience proves that every operator should adopt one of two methods: Either cut losses short, or take an investment position. We propose to point out today some of the advantages of cutting losses short.

The buyer of any stock has some reason for his action. He has heard that the stock is going up; he believes that it is selling below its value, he sees that a bull market is under way and believes that this stock will go up as much as any other. These and similar reasons lead to buying.

It is obvious that in all but one of these cases the buyer does not profess to know anything definitely about the stock he buys. He acts on the suggestions or advice of others. Points are good when they are good, and under some conditions can very wisely be followed. There is nothing better in trading than to know that a great operator or a great syndicate intends for good reasons to move the price of a stock from a lower to a higher figure.

But almost everybody learns by sad experience that the

"best laid plans of mice and men gang aft agley." Great operators change their minds about the expediency of market movements and most of them have learned that it is one thing to will and another to do in stock speculation. Hence the trader who takes a point, even from good sources, has only partial assurance of profitable results.

His true protection in such a case lies in a stop order. If the price advances, well and good, but if it declines his stop order cuts his loss short, while those who do not stop the loss, but who listen to assurances that the market is all right, often see larger losses in the end.

The general rule is to stop losses within a range of two or three points from the purchase price. All purchases on points, tendencies and rumors should be regarded as guesses and protected by stop orders. Traders, looking over their accounts, seldom lament the losses of $200, which they find scattered through their books as the result of stops, but they deeply lament the $1,500 or the $2,500 losses which reflect overconfidence in a position which proved unsound.

The difficulty with stop orders is that they are frequently exercised when the event shows that the loss need not have been taken. There is no help for this, but the placing of a stop order can be wisely varied by the circumstances of a given case. Suppose that the 5-year movement showed a bull market to be in progress; that there has come in this advance a 5-point reaction in a stock like Union Pacific and that a purchase had been made 5 points from the previous highest.

If the price declined 2 points more in such a case, it would probably be wise to exercise the stop order as the fall would suggest a down swing of larger proportions than had been anticipated. It might be such a move as occurred in December, 1899, when stop orders proved exceedingly profitable in bull accounts. If the price subsequently recovered the 2 points, and the stock was repurchased at about the original price, it would probably be wise to put the stop order the next time about 3 points away, under a belief that the stock would not go quite so low as it went before and that the stop order would therefore not be executed.

If this reasoning proved sound, and the price advanced, the stop order could wisely be kept 3 points below the market price until the stock had advanced several points and showed signs of what is called "toppiness." Then it might be well to advance the stop order to 2 points and await developments. The stop order is of primary importance when a purchase is first made and when its wisdom is in doubt. It is also of primary importance in pyramiding; that is, where stock is being bought on an advancing market every point up, because in such a case the stop order is relied upon to prevent the turning of a profit into a loss. It is of importance when a stock has had its normal swing for the purpose of saving most of the profit if a reaction comes, while leaving a chance open for further advance. It is of least importance when a stock has been well bought and is slowly advancing. It should be set further away from the market at such a time than any other so as to avoid being caught on the small setbacks which occur in an advancing period.

By means of a stop order, an operator can trade freely in active stocks of uncertain value, which he would not venture to touch as an investment. By it, he can trade in much larger amounts than he could otherwise undertake to protect. The stop order is the friend of the active speculator, who wants to make a quick dash for a large profit and who is willing to make small losses in the hope of getting a good run once in four or five attempts. It is the friend of the small operator, the out-of-town operator and the timid operator. It should be applied, however, only in active stocks where there is a large market. Stop orders should not be given in inactive stocks, as the seller may be slaughtered in their execution.

A stop order to sell 100 shares of Union Pacific at 75 means that the stock must be sold at the best price obtainable as soon as there has been a transaction at 75. If the best price were 74 or 73, it would still be the duty of the broker to sell. Hence the importance of not giving such orders in stocks where wide differences in quotations may be expected.

Selling Short

I N PICKING OUT a stock to sell short, the first consideration ought to be that the price is above value, and that future value appears to be shrinking. It should be an active stock and, if possible, a stock of large capital. It should be an old stock by preference, which means having wide distribution instead of concentrated ownership. By preference it should be a high-priced stock with a reasonable probability that dividends will be reduced or passed.

Such a stock should be sold on advances and bought on moderate declines, say 4 or 5 points, as long as the market seems to be reasonably steady. But, if the market becomes distinctly weak, only part of the short stock should be bought in with the hope that some short interest may be established at a price so high as to be out of reach of temporary swings. **The best profits in the stock market are made by people who get long or short at extremes and stay for months or years before they take their profit.**

23

SAMUEL
A. NELSON

Author and Dow Theory Compiler

It is generally agreed that the man who first compiled
Charles Dow's writings and thus "launched" the Dow
Theory, was S. A. Nelson. However Nelson's image has
been somewhat smothered by that reputation, for his
writings on trading tactics offer a great deal, apart from
Dow concepts. It is this more or less unknown side of
Nelson that is presented here. Adequate coverage of
Dow's views can be found elsewhere in this volume, but
only here can we present the real S. A. Nelson.

It was shortly after Dow's death that Nelson wrote his
ABC of Wall Street and the *ABC of Stock Speculation.*
In 1907 he wrote *The Consolidated Stock Exchange of
New York.*

He tried to get Dow to write a book on Dow's ideas
and when he failed to persuade him, Nelson wrote it himself, compiling all he could find of what Dow had said on
stock speculation in *The Wall Street Journal.*

Very little biographical information is available on
Nelson. He was described as a conscientious and sensible
little man, one whom his co-workers both liked and
laughed at for they could not take him quite as seriously
as he took himself.

He was slowly dying of tuberculosis at the time of his
most important writing (1902 to 1907) and died not long

thereafter, a great distance from the Wall Street he loved.

Though some called him a pathetic, sickly, little figure with an earnest and strained face, he was active and vibrant with his pen, as the following pages reveal, and it was he who coined the term "Dow's Theory."

The Wisdom of

SAMUEL A. NELSON

A Trader's Apprenticeship

THE SUCCESSFUL TRADER is obliged to serve an apprenticeship as a trader. This usually requires 6-12 months of close application. It is almost a tradition that novices who plunge successfully in the first year are very often failures in the second or third year. Early success is misleading and deceptive. A queer thing about this trade is that you may acquire it very slowly and gradually or you may stick at it and work away for months when suddenly in the most mysterious way the whole thing opens up to you and what seemed very difficult becomes comparatively simple. **You learn by a process of elimination.** You are bound to make mistakes. In some instances it takes quite a long time to find out that three profits of $25 each do not balance a loss of $100.

As to whether the work is harder and more dangerous than other trades . . . why no. It all depends on the man.

The object of all business is the "making of money" and nothing else. Wall Street is certainly no different from any other place or center of business activity, in this respect.

A healthy skepticism is seldom out of place in Wall

Street, so far as speculation is concerned. Money is very seldom lost thereby. People who have had experience covering one or two panics know very well that the first lesson that has to be learned by the successful speculator is the avoidance of the disaster always caused by a panic. The very essence of a panic is that it sweeps away everyone who is overtrading—whether it be to a large or to a small extent. Of what use is it to pile up imposing paper profits if they are all to be swept away when the tidal wave strikes? The only way whereby people can avoid being caught in a panic is by the exercise at all times of great conservatism and considerable skepticism. The successful speculator must be content at times to ignore probably two out of every three apparent opportunities to make money, and must know how to sell and take his profits when the "bull" chorus is loudest. When he has learned that much, he has learned a great deal.

Speculative Fever

TO STAND IN the office of a commission firm all day
and hear the market opinions expressed and the
reasons for making commitments is to understand
why so much money is lost. The man who "guesses," who
has a "fancy for a particular stock," "who wishes to make
a bit," who has "a tip," is in the majority. He has the
speculative fever, and having contracted the disease he
has not the time nor the mood to adopt the reasoning
dictated by ordinary common sense.

"Buy," says a customer to his broker, "100 shares of
Metropolitan at 150."

The stock is bought at a cash cost of $15,000. The cus-
tomer's equity in the stock is $1,000. The stock is capable
of wide fluctuations.

"What did you buy it on?" the customer is asked.

"My friend Smith told me that it is going up."

"Who is Smith?"

"Oh, a neighbor of mine. He heard it was a good thing
from Jones, whose cousin is a director in the company."

Would this man, who is a type, have invested $15,000

(equity $1,000) in his own business (mercantile) without a most careful investigation of conditions, and consequences, profits and losses, present and prospective? Would Smith and Jones influence him in such a transaction? Certainly not. And yet thousands of stock market ventures are made annually without any more justification.

Therefore if about to speculate in stocks, it behooves you to ask yourself if you possess the temperament and accurate and swift reasoning powers necessary to cope with the ablest money getters in the world. If you do, you will find that hardly a day passes that Wall Street does not present great opportunities for your skill in money making.

Market Panics

PANICS IN THE stock market have a well defined course. The record since 1873 shows only two exceptions to the rule, the rule prevailing in all other cases. A panicky market usually lasts during parts of three days, although this is not invariable. The lowest prices are usually made on the second day. From those prices there is a recovery amounting usually to more than half the amount of the decline from the level of prices prevailing before the panic. This recovery culminates within a week and sometimes not for thirty days, but in all cases prior to the May 9, 1901 panic, within thirty days. After that comes a slow decline during which prices lose at least half of their recovery and in case of a bear market all the recovery and more is lost.

Nothing is more common than to hear people say that the big bankers can do what they please with the stock market, and yet nothing is further from the truth. The stock market is in the end made by the public and by no one else, if the smaller fluctuations and minor "swings" be disregarded. Traders can move prices within narrow limits; bankers can move them within wider limits, but without the public the market tends constantly to equilibrium. Stocks go off when traders sell and rally when they cover; stocks advance when bankers bid them up, but decline unless the public buys on the advance. Both traders and bankers can and generally do anticipate the public in its operations, but if the public does not do what is expected of it nothing is gained thereby.

The investor determines the prices of stocks in the long run. This statement is sometimes disputed by those who point to the fluctuations which are confessedly made by manipulators without regard to value. It is true that such fluctuations occur, but when the manipulation is over the voice of the investor is again heard. If he decides that a given stock is worth only so much, the manipulator will ultimately be compelled to accept that valuation because manipulation cannot be kept up. The object of manipulation is to buy below value and sell above value. The experience of all traders will afford many illustrations of how stocks have recovered after artificial depression and relapsed after artificial advances to the middle point which represented value as it was understood by those who bought or held as investors.

The Role of Value

VALUE HAS LITTLE to do with temporary fluctuations in stock prices, **but is the determining factor in the long run.** Values when applied to stocks are determined in the end by the return to the investor, and nothing is more certain than that the investor establishes the price of stocks. The manipulator is all-powerful for a time. He can mark prices up or down. He can mislead investors, inducing them to buy when he wishes to sell, and to sell when he wishes to buy; but manipulation in a stock cannot be permanent, and in the end the investor learns the approximate truth. His decision to keep his stock or to sell it then makes a price independent of speculation and, in a large sense, indicative of true value. It is so indicative because the price made is well known to insiders, who also know better than anyone else the true value of the stock. If the price is too low, the insiders will buy; hence stability is the price of a stock means that insiders do not think the stock especially cheap or dear.

The reason why in a bull market, dullness is followed by advance, is that a bull market is the exponent of increasing values. Values go on increasing, while the market rests, and prices start up because it becomes apparent to cliques or individuals that values are above prices, and that there is margin for use. Exactly the reverse argument applies to declines after dullness in a bear period.

Prices fall because values are falling, and dullness merely allows the fall in value to get ahead of the fall in prices. The start after a period of inactivity is generally due either to some special event or to manipulation. In the former case, the reason for acting is obvious. In the latter case, manipulators begin by studying the situation and reach a conclusion that it will pay them to move prices.

They then scrutinize the speculative situation, and learn something of the position of traders; whether they are carrying a good many stocks or not; whether they seem disposed to deal; whether margins appear to be large or small; and whether specialists have large scale orders to either buy or sell. This gives a basis on which manipulation begins. The public often follows the lead given, sometimes to its own advantage and sometimes to the advantage of the manipulators. All this, however, is merely an incident in the main tendency of prices, which, as a whole, is in accord with the values which grow out of changes in earnings. Temporary movements in the market should always be considered with reference to their bearing on the main movement. The great mistake made by the public is paying attention to prices instead of values.

Whoever knows that the value of a particular stock is rising under conditions which promise stability, and the absence of developments calculated to neutralize the effect of increasing earnings, should buy that stock whenever it declines in sympathy with other stocks, and hold it until the price is considered high enough for the value as it is believed to exist.

This implies study and knowledge of the stock chosen, but this marks the difference between intelligent trading and mere gambling. Anybody can guess whether a stock will go up or down, but it is only guessing and the cost of guessing will eat up most of the net profits of trading on pure guesses. Intelligent trading begins with study of conditions, and a justified opinion that the general situation is either growing better or worse.

If general conditions are improving, ascertain if the particular stock to be dealt in is having a fair share of that general improvement. Is its value rising? If so, determine whether the price of the stock is low or high with reference to that value. If it is low, buy the stock and wait. Do not be discouraged if it does not move. The more value goes on increasing, the greater the certainty that rise in the stock will come. When it does come, do not take two or three points profit and then wait for a reaction, but consider whether the stock is still cheap at the advance, and if so, buy more, rather than sell under the assumption that the expected rise is under way. Keep the stock until the price appears to be up to the value and get a substantial profit. This is the way the large operators make their money; not by trading back and forth, but by accurate forecasts of coming changes in value, and then buying stocks in quantity and putting the price up to value. The small operator cannot put prices up, but if his premises are sound, he can hold stock with assurance that large operators and investors will put the price up for him.

The Universal Laws of Speculation

A CLOSE STUDENT of speculation in all its forms as conducted on the exchanges of this country has arrived at the following conclusions, which, he says, in application to speculation are "universal laws." He divides his conclusions into two groups, laws absolute and laws conditional.

LAWS ABSOLUTE

1. Never overtrade. To take an interest larger than the capital justifies, is to invite disaster. With such an interest, a fluctuation in the market unnerves the operator, and his judgment becomes worthless.

2. Never "double up"; that is, never completely and at once reverse a position. Being "long," for instance, do not "sell out" and go as much "short." This may occasionally succeed, but is very hazardous, for should the market begin again to advance, the mind reverts to its original opinion and the speculator "covers up" and "goes long" again. Should this last change be wrong, complete demoralization ensues. The change in the original position should have been made moderately, cautiously, thus keeping the judgment clear and preserving the balance of mind.

3. **"Run quick"** or not at all; that is to say, act promptly at the first approach of danger, but failing to do this until others see the danger hold on or close out part of the "interest."

4. **Another rule is,** when doubtful **reduce the amount of the interest;** for either the mind is not satisfied with the position taken, or the interest is too large for safety. One man told another that he could not sleep on account of his position in the market; his friend judiciously and laconically replied: **"Sell down to the sleeping point."**

RULES CONDITIONAL

These rules are subject to modification, according to the circumstances, individuality and temperament of the speculator.

It is better to "average up" (pyramiding) than to "average down." This opinion is contrary to the one commonly held and acted upon; it being the practice to buy and on a decline buy more. This reduces the average. Probably four times out of five this method will result in striking a reaction in the market that will prevent loss, but the fifth time, meeting with a permanently declining market, the operator loses his head and closes out, making a heavy loss—a loss so great as to bring complete demoralization, often ruin.

But "buying up" is the reverse of the method just explained; that is to say, buying at first moderately and as the market advances adding slowly and cautiously to the "line." This is a way of speculating that requires great care and watchfulness, for the market will often (probably four times out of five) react to the point of "average." **Here lies the danger. Failure to close out at the point of average destroys the safety of the whole operation.**

WILLIAM P. HAMILTON

Pioneer Technician, and Successor to Dow

Famous as the man whose October 25, 1929 *Wall Street Journal* editorial "The Turn of the Tide" correctly identified the termination of the great bull market of the 1920's, William Peter Hamilton considerably furthered the theory first evolved by Charles Dow with thorough organization and formulation of the leading concepts.

Born in England and trained there as a newspaperman, he arrived in America in 1899 and joined *The Wall Street Journal* that same year. There is no proof that Hamilton was ever a close intimate of Dow, his editor, but rather the evidence points to relationship of employer and employee, or editor and reporter. Five years after Dow's death Hamilton became editor of *The Wall Street Journal*, where, in addition to taking up where Dow left off in the field of technical stock market interpretation, he undertook to expound Dow's views in an organized manner, which became "The Dow Theory."

To Hamilton should go much credit, because Dow did not deliberately set forth his ideas for use as a market tool. Dow used the market to predict business; but Hamilton put together these various findings for use as a method of predicting the stock market, which for investors was probably more to the point.

Hamilton had a better score of hits and misses than

many modern day market analysts. His only notable miscalculation was in 1926 when he incorrectly announced that a bear market was at hand, which turned out later to have been a severe secondary reaction instead.

He was able to pass sound judgment upon the action of the stock market for almost three decades until his death in 1929, with his views constantly in the public eye through the medium of his articles in *The Wall Street Journal*. That he was able to do this speaks a testimony of the highest eloquence.

Hamilton wrote an incisive book in 1922, entitled *The Stock Market Barometer*, in which he formed Dow's ideas and his own into just what his book calls itself—a "barometer," by which stock market weather was predicted. This book has come to be regarded as the "Bible" of the Dow Theory.

The Wisdom of
WILLIAM P. HAMILTON

Dow's Theory, Applied to Speculation

WE HAVE SEEN in past discussions of Dow's theory of the stock-market price movement that the essence of it could be summed up in three sentences. In an editorial published December 19, 1900, he says, in *The Wall Street Journal:*

"The market is always to be considered as having three movements, all going on at the same time. The first is the narrow movement from day to day. The second is the short swing, running from two weeks to a month or more; the third is the main movement, covering at least four years in its duration."

It has already been shown that his third and main movement may complete itself in much less than Dow's assumed four years, and also how an attempt to divide the ten-year period of the panic cycle theory into a bear and bull market of approximately five years each led to an unconscious exaggeration. That, however, is immaterial. Dow had successfully formulated a theory of the market movements of the highest value, and had synchronized those movements so that those who came after him could construct a business barometer.

This is the essence of Dow's theory, and it need hardly be said that he did not see, or live to see, all that it implied. He never wrote a single editorial on the theory alone, but returns to it to illustrate his discussions on stock-market speculation, and the underlying facts and truths responsible not only for speculation (using the word in its best and most useful sense) but for the market itself.

It is not surprising that *The Wall Street Journal* received many inquiries as to the assumptions it made on the basis of Dow's major premise. On January 4, 1902, Dow replies to a pertinent question, and any thoughtful reader of these pages should be able to answer it himself. The correspondent asks him, "For some time you have been writing rather bullish on the immediate market, yet a little bearish in a larger sense. How do you make this consistent?" Dow's reply was, of course, that he was bullish after the secondary swing but that he did not think, in view of stock values from earnings of record, that a bull market which had then been operative sixteen months could run much further. It was a curious contraction, incidentally, of his own minimum four-year estimate, but that major upward swing as a matter of fact ran until the following September. It may be said that such a swing always outruns values. **In its final stage it is discounting possibilities only.**

In the same editorial Dow goes on to give a useful definition from which legitimate inferences may be drawn. He says:

"It is a bull period as long as the average of one high point exceeds that of previous high points. It is a bear period when the low point becomes lower than the previous low points. It is often difficult to judge whether the end of an advance has come because the movement of prices is that which would occur if the main tendency had changed. Yet, it may only be an unusually pronounced secondary movement."

This passage contains, by implication, both the idea of "double tops" and "double bottoms" (which I frankly confess I have not found essential or greatly useful) and the idea of a "line," as shown in the narrow fluctuation of the averages over a recognized period, necessarily one either of accumulation or distribution. This has been found to be of the greatest service in showing the further persistence of the main movement, or the possible termination of the secondary movement, so apt to be mistaken for the initiation of a new major trend.

It has been said before that Dow's theory is in no sense to be regarded as a gambler's system for beating the game. Any trader would disregard it at his peril, but Dow himself never considered it in that light, as I can testify from many discussions with him . . . It would perhaps be well to point out here that a knowledge of the major movement of the market, whether up or down, is necessary for the successful flotation of any largely capitalized enterprise.

It is essentially the business of a barometer to predict. In that lies its great value, and in that lies the value of Dow's Theory. The stock market is the barometer of the country's and even the world's business, and the theory shows how to read it . . . **The sum and tendency of the transactions in the Stock Exchange represent the sum of all Wall Street's knowledge of the past, immediate and remote, applied to the discounting of the future.** There is no need to add to the averages, as some statisticians do, elaborate compilations of commodity price index numbers, bank clearings, fluctuations in exchange, volume of domestic and foreign trade or anything else. Wall Street considers all these things. It properly regards them as experience of the past, if only of the immediate past to be used for estimating the future. They are merely creating causes of the weather predicted.

The Nature of Secondary Swings

PREVIOUS DISCUSSIONS HAVE shown how it was possible successfully to diagnose a major swing in its incipient stages. But the **secondary** movement postulated in Dow's Theory is a different matter. We have proved by analysis the correctness of the theory of the market as containing three distinct and, in a way, simultaneous movements—the great primary swing up or down; the secondary movement, represented by reactions in a bull market and corresponding rallies in a bear market; and the daily fluctuation. It may be that this discussion will seem to be addressed more to the speculator or embryo investor than to those who consider using the stock market barometer as a guide and warning to business.

It may be conceded at once that if it is hard to call the turn of a great bear or bull market it is still harder to say when a secondary movement is due, although there are no insuperable difficulties in the way of showing the termination of the secondary movement and the resumption of the main market trend. We cannot dogmatize about the depth of such movements, in duration or extent. We have seen, from a study of what was really a secondary reaction in a bull market aggravated by the San Francisco calamity in 1906, that such a reaction can look deceptively like the real thing—the development of a new major swing. It can look so vigorous and convincing, as in the case of the Northern Pacific panic of 1901, that even experienced traders will rashly assume that the bull market is over.

Dow estimated the length of a counter movement at from forty to sixty days, but subsequent experience has shown that this longer range is exceedingly rare and that the duration may be appreciably less than forty days. The daily fluctuation might be so considerable as to constitute almost a secondary reaction in itself, if the extent of it were all we were considering. When it was known that the government would take over the railroads, at the end of December, 1917, there was an advance in a single day in the railroad average of over six points. There have been true secondary movements which did not carry even so far as this. It is a tried rule, which will help to guide us in studying the secondary movement, that the change in the broad general direction of the market is abrupt, while the resumption of the major movement is appreciably slower. The latter is frequently foretold by a line of accumulation in a bull market or a line of distribution in a bear market.

Dow's Theory True of All Stock Markets

THE LAW THAT governs the movement of the stock market, formulated here, would be equally true of the London Stock Exchange, the Paris Bourse or even the Berlin Boerse. But we may go further. The principles underlying that law would be true if those Stock Exchanges and ours were wiped out of existence. They would come into operation again, automatically and inevitably, with the re-establishment of a free market in securities in any great Capital. So far as I know, there has not been a record corresponding to the Dow-Jones averages kept by any of the London financial publications. But the stock market there would have the same quality of forecast which the New York market has if similar data were available.

It would be possible to compile from the London Stock Exchange list two or more representative groups of stocks and show their primary, their secondary and their daily movements over the period of years covered by Wetenhall's list and the London Stock Exchange official list. An average made up of the prices of the British railroads might well confirm our own. There is in London a longer and more diversified list of industrial stocks to draw upon. The averages of the South African mining stocks in the Kaffir market, properly compiled from the first Transvaal gold rush in 1889, would have an interest all their own. They would show how gold mining tends to flourish when other industries are stagnant or even prostrated. The comparison of that average with the movement of securities held for fixed income would be highly instructive to the economist. It would demonstrate in the most vivid way the relation of the purchasing power of gold to bonds held for investment. It would prove conclusively the axiom that the price of securities held for fixed income is in inverse ratio to the cost of living, as we shall see for ourselves in a later chapter.

The San Francisco Earthquake

THE YEAR 1906 presents an interesting problem of an arrested main bull movement or an accentuated secondary reaction, according to the way you look at it. It has been said that major bull markets and bear markets alike tend to overrun themselves. If the stock market were omniscient it would protect itself against this over-inflation or over-liquidation, as it automatically protects itself against everything which it can possibly foresee. But we must concede that, even when we have allowed for the further established fact that the stock market represents the sum of all available knowledge about the conditions of business and the influences which affect business, **it cannot protect itself against what it cannot foresee.** It could not foresee the San Francisco earthquake of April 18, 1906, or the subsequent devastating fire.

The Wall Street Barometer...

(Written June 29, 1906)

SPECULATION IS ESSENTIAL not merely in the market for stocks but in any market. Somebody must take chances. The pound of coffee sold across the counter contains greater or less profit to the retailer as he judges the wholesale market correctly. Every market must therefore adjust itself not merely to present conditions but to future conditions. In this respect stocks are like any other commodity, but they cover so wide a range of interests that a general movement in them may, and frequently does, reflect a change in general conditions outside.

In this respect the Wall Street market is something of a rational barometer. It is the constant phrase of the street that a movement is over "when the news is out." Stockholders and intelligent speculators operate not on what everybody knows, but on what they alone know or intelligently anticipate. We have often had the spectacle of a general decline in the market, only followed six months afterwards by a contraction in business, or a general advance in the market anticipating by an equal time improving industrial conditions not then obvious.

It is the business of Wall Street to sell securities to the public. Wall treet anticipates that when the business improvement it expects matures, the public will take stocks off its hands. This is really what stablishes a bull market. Favorable conditions inside and out of Wall treet act and interact until the necessary impetus for a stock boom is leveloped. In the summer of 1904 when the unskilled observer was convinced that the McKinley boom was over and industry on the down grade, professional Wall Street was buying stocks. It correctly estimated he vast recuperative power of business. The average price of twenty ctive railroad stocks advanced nearly thirty points in that year with a ontinuous gain between the latter part of May and the beginning of December.

It must always be remembered, however, that there is a main current n the stock market, with innumerable cross currents, eddies, and backwaters, any one of which may be mistaken for a day, a week, or even longer period for the main stream. The market is a barometer. There s no movement in it which has not a meaning. That meaning is sometimes not disclosed until long after the movement takes place, and is till oftener never known at all; but it may truly be said that every movement is reasonable if only the knowledge of its source is complete.

What the barometer needs of course is expert reading. At the present ime the stock market, which, touching the highest point ever recorded on January 22 of this year, has made an irregular reaction. The decline t one time extended in the case of twenty active railroads to over eighteen points, and in the case of twelve active industrials, to almost s much. Even now after very substantial rallies the market has worked off from the recovery point of last April and is even six points below he best quotation of the current month. On the surface, crop prospects, industrial conditions and the money market are all as favorable s ever. Here is an opportunity for the amateur reader of the barometer. s the market, or is it not, reflecting some change in fundamental conditions which shall justify the present quotations six months hence?

Causes of the 1907 Panic

T HESE BEAR ARGUMENTS were given on March 15 1907, and they read curiously now. (1922) They were:

"1. Excessive prosperity.

2. High cost of living, due largely to the effect upon prices of a great gold production.

3. Readjustment of values to the higher rates of interest

4. Speculation in land absorbing liquid capital that might otherwise be available for commercial enter prises.

5. Roosevelt and his policy of government regulation of the corporations.

6. Anti-railroad agitation in the various states.

7. Progress of socialistic sentiment and demagogic attacks on wealth.

8. Harriman investigation of exposure of bad practices in high finance.

9. War between big financial interests.

10. Over-production of securities.

11. Effect of San Francisco earthquake."

There were other causes quoted of only momentary consequence, in which possible bear manipulation was put last. It has been said already that there never was a bear market which was not justified by the facts subsequently disclosed. Are we not entitled to say that some of these influences became permanent, to an extent which even the stock market could not possibly foresee, conceding that it is, at least theoretically, of longer and larger vision than any of us? As after events proved, the over-regulation of the railroads alone was sufficient to justify investors in protecting themselves, whatever the consequences to the stock market might be.

In retrospect, the year 1907 seems to be the most interesting I have ever spent in Wall Street, and perhaps the most instructive. It is full of lessons and warnings.

(Editor's Note: *The following piece, from* The Wall Street Journal *of October 25, 1929, in Hamilton's most celebrated editorial, the one in which he announced that the 1929-1932 bear market had been confirmed by major Dow Theory signals, and giving a hint of the depression that was to come. The article was greeted with great disbelief by the boom-conditioned public of that day, most of whom thought that the market surely must be close to bottoming out after its violent slide of September and October. Later events, however, proved Hamilton's historic pronouncement was well-founded though he underestimated the scope of the coming business contraction.)*

A Turn in the Tide

ON THE LATE Charles H. Dow's well known method of reading the stock market movement from the Dow-Jones averages, the twenty railroad stocks on Wednesday, October 23 confirmed a bearish indication given by the industrials two days before. Together the averages gave the signal for a bear market in stocks after a major bull market with the unprecedented duration of almost six years. It is noteworthy that Barron's and the Dow-Jones NEWS service on October 21 pointed out the significance of the industrial signal, given subsequent confirmation by the railroad average. The comment was as follows:

"If, however, the market broke again, after a failure to pass the old highs, and the decline carried the price of the industrials below 325.17 and the railroads below 168.26, the bearish indication would be strong, and might well represent something more than a secondary reaction, however severe. It has often been said in these studies of the price movement that the barometer never indicates duration. There was a genuine major bear market in 1923, but it lasted only eight months. One good reason for not taking the present indications too seriously is that they have all been recorded in a most unusually short space of time. The severest reaction from the high point of the year had just one month's duration. In view of the nationwide character of the speculation, this seems a dangerously short period to infer anything like complete reversal in public sentiment."

There was a striking consistency about the market movement since the high figure of September 3. There were at least four rallies in the course of the decline in the industrials before the definite new low point was established and each of these was weaker than the last. Dow always considered this a danger signal, but for the past thirty years it has been the custom in discussing the stock market as a barometer of business to require that one average should confirm the other. Failure to agree has been found deceptive.

There are people trading in Wall Street, and many all over the country who have never seen a real bear market, as for instance, that which began in October, 1919, and lasted for two years, or that from 1912 to 1914 which predicted the Great War if the world had then been able to interpret the signs. What is more material is that the stock market does forecast the general business of the country. The big bull market was confirmed by six years of prosperity and if the stock market takes the other direction there will be contraction in business later, although on present indications only in moderate volume.

Some time ago it was said in a *Wall Street Journal* editorial that if the stock market was compelled to deflate, as politicians seemed so earnestly to wish, they would shortly after experience a deflation elsewhere which would be much less to their liking.

Insiders Are Poor Traders

THESE SO-CALLED "INSIDERS," the real men who conduct the real business of a corporation, are too busy to spend their time over the stock ticker. They are far too limited, too restricted to their particular trade, to be good judges of the turn of the market. They are normally bullish on their own property, in the respect that they believe it to be a growing concern with great possibilities. But of the fluctuations of business which will affect their stock, together with the rest in the same group or all other railroad and industrial stocks in the same market, their view is singularly limited. It is not mere cynicism but truth to say that **sufficient inside information can ruin anybody in Wall Street.**

High Volume in Bull Markets

IT IS WORTH while to note that the volume of trading is always larger in a bull than in a bear market. It expands as prices go up and contracts as they decline. A moment's thought will reveal the reason. When the market has been under long depression many people have lost money, actually and on paper, and the fund for speculation or speculative investment is correspondingly contracted. On the advance, however, many people are making money, actually and on paper, and the well nigh universal experience has been that in the last stages of a bull market they trade in stocks beyond their real resources. This is uniformly true of major bull swings, but is subject to great modification in the secondary movements. A sharp reaction in a bull market will often stimulate the volume of business.

Averages No Blabbermouth

T HE DOW JONES averages . . . have a discretion not shared by all the prophets. They are not talking all the time.

Labor Versus Brains

W E KNOW NOW that, far from labor creating everything (the preposterous major premise of Karl Marx) labor creates only a fraction of the sum of human wealth compared with the product of brains.

ROBERT RHEA

Dow Historian and Record-Keeper

Robert Rhea, the third in a line of celebrated Dow disciples, was born in 1896 in Nashville, Tennessee. His father ran a river boat line on the Mississippi, loved the stock market, and had been rich and poor, alternately, several times.

Before Robert was out of school his father gave him W. P. Hamilton's *Wall Street Journal* editorials on Dow Theory, and told him "to master them or get spanked."

After a short stay in college, Robert started a river boat line that nearly ran his father's out of business. He carried his savings in his pocket. On his father's advice he sent his funds to Henry Clews in New York with instructions to buy some good stock, and 10 shares of U. S. Steel were purchased at 14. This transaction was the start of Rhea's real interest in stocks; thereafter, he subscribed to *The Wall Street Journal*.

Later, Robert contracted tuberculosis and went to Colorado. But tuberculosis didn't prevent Rhea from enlisting in the Air Corps in 1917. His plane crashed, however, a piece of propeller pierced a lung, and Rhea returned to Colorado a permanent invalid.

In bed he began to average and chart stock prices and study Dow Theory again. He found he could forget his physical pain by concentrating heavily on this work so that at the day's end he was exhausted and could sleep.

When Hamilton died in 1929 the Dow Jones Company needed a new "high priest" for the Dow cult and published some of Rhea's "notebooks" in *Barron's*. The next year Rhea put his ideas on Dow lore into a book, and when publishers refused to print it, he published it himself and sold over 90,000 copies.

Letters began to stack up at the foot of his bed. Unable to answer them individually, he mailed a notice that if and when he had anything to say, he would mimeograph it and send it to anyone who wanted it.

By 1938 Rhea was selling his mimeographed "Dow Theory Comments" opinions to 5,000 clients at $40 a year. Soon he had 25 assistants and his bedroom became a statistical storehouse. He did **not** want to be a tipster; however, he reputedly averaged $436 gain as against every $100 he lost. He often composed tirades against Franklin D. Roosevelt, which were included at no extra charge in his letters.

Rhea wrote three books: *Dow's Theory Applied to Business and Banking* in 1938, *The Dow Theory* in 1932, and *The Story of the Averages* in 1932 published by Rhea, Greiner & Co.; in connection with the last-named work he compiled a book of graphic charts of the daily Dow Jones Averages from their commencement.

Rhea died in 1939, at the age of 43.

The Wisdom of
ROBERT RHEA

Determining the Trend

SUCCESSIVE RALLIES penetrating preceding high points, with ensuing declines terminating above preceding low points, offer a bullish indication. Conversely, failure of the rallies to penetrate previous high points, with ensuing declines carrying below former low points, is bearish. Inferences so drawn are useful in appraising secondary reactions and are of major importance in forecasting the resumption, continuation, or change of the primary trend. For the purpose of this discussion, a rally or a decline is defined as one or more daily movements resulting in a net reversal of direction exceeding three per cent of the price of either average. Such movements have but little authority unless confirmed in direction by both averages, but the confirmation need not occur on the same day.

The significance of rallies in a secondary reaction in a bull market is explained by Hamilton as follows: ". . . On the well-tested rule of reading the averages, a major bull swing continues so long as the rally from a secondary reaction establishes new high points in both averages, not necessarily on the same day, or even in the same week, provided only that they confirm each other." (Dec. 30, 1921)

It should always be remembered that a new high or low by one average, unconfirmed by the other, is deceptive. Such action frequently denotes a change of a secondary nature, although sometimes proving to be of primary importance.

The authority of new highs or lows which are properly confirmed remains in force until cancelled by some later definite confirmed action. If, for instance, new highs are made in a primary bull market, the prediction is valid that the bull market will continue for a considerable time. Moreover, if one average later retraces its advance to a point below its old high, or even below a previous low point, but the other average fails to confirm the action, it is proper to infer that the previous bullish indication is still in force. Hamilton explains this as follows: "The barometer does not give indications every day and all the time; according to Charles H. Dow's theory, an indication remains in force until it is cancelled by another, or re-inforced in some way, as, for instance, when the industrial average confirms the railroad average or vice versa." (Sept. 23, 1929)

If, after a severe secondary reaction in a primary bull market, the ensuing rallies fail to go to new highs within a reasonable time and a further drastic decline occurs extending below the low points of the previous reaction, it is generally safe to assume the primary trend has changed from bullish to bearish. Conversely, when, after a decline has carried both averages to new low ground in a bear market, an important secondary reaction has taken place and the next decline fails to carry either average to a new low, one may infer that the primary trend has changed from bear to bull if the next rally carries both averages above the high points of the last important rally. Few exceptions to this rule can be found in the charted averages when examined over a 35-year period.

Many traders try to apply this rule to minor reactions, forgetting that a normal secondary reaction generally lasts from three to 12 weeks and retraces from one-third to two-thirds of the primary movement since the last important secondary reaction. The best way for the students to gain a complete understanding of the significance of small rallies and declines is to study the charted daily movements over the entire record of the averages.

According to Hamilton, "Dow always ignored a movement of one average which was not confirmed by the other, and experience since his death has shown the wisdom of that method of checking the reading of the averages. His theory was that a downward movement of secondary, and perhaps ultimately primary, importance was established when the new lows for both averages were under the low points of the preceding reaction." (June 25, 1928)

Because a lucid explanation of the significance of rallies and declines was always proved so difficult, and because a proper understanding of the rise and fall of prices as compared to previous similar movements is of such vital importance when using the averages as a forecasting device, it is perhaps wise to offer a second quotation which is merely a repetition, although phrased differently: "Whenever a series of rallies and declines have occurred in the day to day movement, always confirmed by both rail and industrial averages, and the rallies carry above immediately preceding high points, with declines failing to penetrate recent lows, the implication is bullish for the immediate future, but not necessarily indicating a primary bull trend."

When a series of such rallies and declines of both averages have penetrated the highest points previously attained in a primary bull market, it is generally safe to infer that the primary bull trend will continue for a considerable period of time. Conversely, successive rallies and declines, with highs failing to penetrate the immediately preceding high points, and the ensuing declines carrying below previous low prices, afford a bearish implication for the immediate future, although not necessary implying a primary bear trend. On the other hand, when a series of rallies and declines break through the lowest prices of a primary bear trend, the probability of much lower prices is generally a reasonable inference. When declines in a primary bull market result in violating the lowest points encountered during the last major secondary reaction of that market, it may generally be assumed that the primary trend has changed from bullish to bearish; the converse, of course, is usually a dependable means of determining when a bear primary movement has changed to the beginning of a bull market.

Occasional exceptions can be found, and it is proper that this should be true, for otherwise these rules would constitute a sure way of beating the stock market. Such a method would, of course, very quickly result in there being no market.

Characteristics of Bull Market Peaks

THE TERMINATION OF a bull market is much harder to recognize than the end of a bear market. At the peak, both averages are, of course, in new high ground. Without exception, bull markets of the past have ended in periods of relatively heavy activity; moreover, near the top, pools have always been active, and comparatively worthless stocks have been advanced rapidly. Eager speculators, inoculated with the virus of greed and excitement, buy anything that is going up, regardless of earnings or of intrinsic worth. Truly, the termination of bull markets represents a period when nothing can justify the prices at which stocks are changing hands except the hope and expectation of those who are suffering from excessive speculative temperature.

When stocks are nearing the peak, call money is sometimes high but at other times it is not particularly so. **It is seldom that anything is apparent in the current business statistical situation to indicate that a collapse is imminent. Almost invariably, the opinions of newspaper writers, services, and brokers are rampantly bullish.**

At first thought it might seem that the conditions described would not be very hard to recognize, but in active practice it proves to be most difficult, for the reason that while more or less uniform conditions, as described, exist at bull peaks, it does not follow that whenever such situations develop a market collapse occurs. It is a case where unhealthy conditions have been gradually building up over the months, and that operator is shrewd indeed who can identify the exact day when public excitement reaches its zenith.

HOW TO AVOID GETTING CAUGHT IN BEAR MARKETS

Without meaning to imply that I am an expert on trading tactics, and with the full consciousness that trading methods which serve one man may appear foolish to another, I shall, nevertheless, try to outline methods which have, on more than one occasion in the past, preserved the greater portion of my modest speculative capital from the ravages of bear markets.

One method of avoiding bear market disaster is to get out of the market when a bull period has run for a normal length of time, **provided speculation is then rampant,** and if a long advance into new primary high ground has taken place without being interrupted by a secondary correction—all this, provided prices appear to have discounted present and future earnings for a great many years to come.

Investors may ask how they can determine the point when stocks are selling far above value and probable earnings. That, indeed, is a hard question to answer because no two men appraise values on the same basis. I can only say that sometime before the peak was reached in 1929, American Telephone and Telegraph common stock was selling around $300 per share. It had a book value of about $128, and its best recorded earnings were in 1929 when the reported net for common was $12.67 per share. Now in 1926 the stock had sold for $151 when its book value was $126, with earnings of $11.95. With its dividend at $9.00, a comparatively small amount was carried to surplus each year. At the price first noted above, the advance in the quoted value of this stock had obviously discounted earnings for many years in the future; moreover, it was selling far above its intrinsic value. Similar conditions existed in the stocks of General Motors, Sears Roebuck, Consolidated Gas, and hundreds of other well-managed corporations, while the price situation in Radio and other such favorites was absurd. These remarks are made only to show how one factor, always existing near the peak, and one which was understood and explained by Hamilton, could be detected by any one understanding elementary arithmetic. This speculator, for one, sold out partly in 1928 and partly in the Spring of 1929. These sales were premature, as later developments showed, but prices received for securities later proved to be most attractive, and, having once retired, I did not again re-enter that market. My next venture was on the short side after the prices had "turned the corner."

I presume that the indications upon which my decision to sell was based might have been said to exist in the Fall of 1927. However, at that time the market was showing no signs whatever of losing any steam.

Short Selling

A S A GENERAL THING, when speculators begin to understand something about primary trends of the stock market, they start to make plans for shorting stocks in bear markets. Few traders have found the short side profitable over a long period of time. I think that more than 75 per cent of my own losses have resulted from short sales.

Many people seem to think that there is something immoral about short selling. I, for one, have always thought that the difference between long and short operations is about the same as the difference between betting on black and red flushes in a poker game, at least so far as morality is concerned.

Perhaps one reason for my frequent bad luck on the short side was the fact that I never really got ahead of the market until I learned to let margin trading alone, but when I short stocks I am conscious of the fact that I am **technically** on margin from the minute the trade is made. You can't take a short transaction out of a broker's office and lock it up in your box, as can be done when long stocks are purchased. The liability behind an investment of $100,000 in stocks is limited to that amount. If declines should occur, the certificates would still be owed. But an "outright" short commitment on $100,000 worth of stocks, backed by $100,000 cash, would be completely wiped out by an advance of 100 per cent. Many old traders have told me that when short they are under a nervous tension which militates against success, and that this strain does not exist when trading for long account.

I have known men who have operated extensively on the short side, but who abandoned that practice without really understanding why their profits were so disappointing. There is a simple arithmetical explanation of this. Consider that a bull buys 100 shares of stock for $10,000, and that the stock advances 100 points. He has made 100 per cent on his capital. Then a bear shorts $10,000 worth of the same stock at $200. The bear will only be short 50 shares. When the stock goes down to $100 again, the bear will have a profit of $5,000 as compared with the $10,000 gained by the bull, notwithstanding the fact that both operators have traded in the same stock over an identical price range, and with the same capital.

A bear shorting a million dollars worth of the Dow-Jones Industrial averages on September 3, 1929, at 381.17, and holding his position until July 8, 1932, when the price was 41.22, would have gained $891,859, or 89.19 per cent, on his capital on an operation extending nearly three years. A bull buying the same stocks on July 8, 1932 with a like amount of capital would have realized the same profit as did the bear, in 49 trading days, when the averages had advanced through 77.98.

In spite of the unfavorable arithmetical odds and other factors, I persist in shorting stocks occasionally, but generally confine operations for a decline to a mere fraction of commitments for long account. If there is any sound reason for fooling with the short side at all, it is the fact that familiarity with and the practice of occasional short selling seem to prevent the development of the bull complex which causes raders to think that stocks are cheap after each decline in bear markets. I had friends during 1930 and 1931 who would never short a stock, and who were so impatient to get into the market that they persisted n buying for an advance in every rally as it occurred. Disaster overtook hem. There is no more certain method of going broke than to make a 1abit of shorting stocks in bull markets or buying for a rally in bear)eriods. Success in both speculation and investment depends upon)ne's ability to swim with the tide rather than against it.

I was so fortunate as to be holding no stocks at the peak in '29 and shortly thereafter carried small short lines intermittently until June, 1932. Without doubt, the short position enabled me to refrain from developing a bull complex during the long decline, and, had I done so, my speculative funds would have been sadly impaired.

The Dow Theorems

THE AVERAGES DISCOUNT EVERYTHING

THE FLUCTUATIONS of the daily closing prices of the Dow-Jones rail and industrial averages afford a composite index of all the hopes, disappointments, and knowledge of everyone who knows anything of financial matters, and for that reason the effects of coming events (excluding acts of God) are always properly anticipated in their movement. The averages quickly appraise such calamities as fires and earthquakes.

THE THEORY IS NOT INFALLIBLE

The Dow theory is not an infallible system for beating the market. Its successful use as an aid in speculation requires serious study, and the summing up of evidence must be impartial. The wish must never be allowed to father the thought.

If these essential elements, around which the theory has been built up, cannot be accepted as axioms, then further study of the subject will prove to be confusing, if not actually misleading.

Reducing the theory to definite **theorems** proved to be a difficult task, but this was done in 1925. Subsequent study together with application of these theorems to trading operations, has not indicated the advisability of altering them now.

DOW'S THREE MOVEMENTS

There are three movements of the averages, all of which may be in progress at one and the same time. The first, and most important, is the primary trend: the broad upward or downward movements known as bull or bear markets, which may be of several years duration. The second, and most deceptive movement, is the secondary reaction: an important decline in a primary bull market or a rally in a primary bear market. These reactions usually last from three weeks to as many months. The third, and usually unimportant, movement is the daily fluctuation.

PRIMARY MOVEMENTS

The primary movement is the broad basic trend generally known as a bull or bear market extending over periods which have varied from less than a year to several years. **The correct determination of the direction of this movement is the most important factor in successful speculation.** There is no known method of forecasting the extent or duration of a primary movement.

PRIMARY BEAR MARKETS

A primary bear market is the long downward movement interrupted by important rallies. It is caused by various economic ills and does not terminate until stock prices have thoroughly discounted the worst that is apt to occur. There are three principal phases of a bear market: the first represents the abandonment of the hopes upon which stocks were purchased at inflated prices; the second reflects selling due to decreased business and earnings, and the third is caused by distress selling of sound securities, regardless of their value, by those who must find a cash market for at least a portion of their assets.

PRIMARY BULL MARKETS

A primary bull market is a broad upward movement interrupted by secondary reactions, and averaging longer than two years. During this time, stock prices advance because of a demand created by both investment and speculative buying caused by improving business conditions and increased speculative activity.

There are three phases of a bull period: the first is represented by reviving confidence in the future of business; the second is the response of stock prices to the known improvement in corporation earnings, and the third is the period when speculation is rampant and inflation apparent—a period when stocks are advanced on hopes and expectations.

SECONDARY REACTIONS

For the purpose of this discussion, a secondary reaction is considered to be an important decline in a bull market or advance in a bear market, usually lasting from three weeks to as many months, during which intervals the price movement generally retraces from 33 per cent to 66 per cent of the primary price change since the termination of the last preceding secondary reaction. These reactions are frequently erroneously assumed to represent a change of primary trend, because obviously the first stage of a bull market must always coincide with a movement which might have proved to have been merely a secondary reaction in a bear market, the contra being true after the peak has been attained in a bull market.

DAILY FLUCTUATIONS

Inferences drawn from one day's movement of the averages are almost certain to be misleading and are of but little value except when "lines" are being formed. The day to day movement must be recorded and studied, however, because a series of charted daily movements always eventually develops into a pattern easily recognized as having a forecasting value.

BOTH AVERAGES MUST CONFIRM

The movements of both the railroad and industrial stock averages should always be considered together. The movement of one price average must be confirmed by the other before reliable inferences may be drawn. Conclusions based upon the movement of one average, unconfirmed by the other, are almost certain to prove misleading.

DETERMINING THE TREND

Successive rallies penetrating preceding high points, with ensuing declines terminating above preceding low points, offer a bullish indication. Conversely, failure of the rallies to penetrate previous high points, with ensuing declines carrying below former low points, is bearish. Inferences so drawn are useful in appraising secondary reactions and are of major importance in forecasting the resumption, continuation, or change of the primary trend. For the purpose of this discussion, a rally or a decline is defined as one or more daily movements resulting in a net reversal of direction exceeding three per cent of the price of either average. Such movements have but little authority unless confirmed in direction by both averages, but the confirmation need not occur on the same day.

LINES

A "line" is a price movement extending two to three weeks or longer, during which period the price variation of both averages move within a range of approximately five per cent. Such a movement indicates either accumulation or distribution. Simultaneous advances above the limits of the "line" indicate accumulation and predict higher prices; conversely, simultaneous declines below the "line" imply distribution and lower prices are sure to follow. Conclusions drawn from the movement of one average, not confirmed by the other, generally prove to be incorrect.

THE RELATION OF VOLUME TO PRICE MOVEMENTS

A market which has been overbought becomes dull on rallies and develops activity on declines; conversely, when a market is oversold, the tendency is to become dull on declines and active on rallies. Bull markets terminate in a period of excessive activity and begin with comparatively light transactions.

DOUBLE TOPS AND DOUBLE BOTTOMS

"Double tops" and "double bottoms" are of but little value in forecasting the price movement and have proved to be deceptive more often than not.

INDIVIDUAL STOCKS

All active and well distributed stocks of great American corporations generally rally and decline with the averages, but any individual stock may reflect conditions not applicable to the average price of any diversified list of stocks.

Points to Remember About Dow's Theory

Number 1. They profit most from Dow's Theory who expect least of it.

2. The Theory is no sure method of beating the market, and no such theory or system will ever be devised.

3. Trading based upon an impartial reading of the averages as implied by the Theory will net frequent losses, but gains will outnumber them to a reasonable extent.

4. Do not try to work the Theory too hard.

5. Do not try to inject innovations until they have been tested over the 37-year record of the averages.

6. Do not try to trade with thin margins and Dow's Theory at the same time.

7. If the Theory is worth following, then study it—learn to form independent opinions, checking them against those of others who have learned to use Dow's methods through several bull and bear cycles.

8. Do not allow your position in the market, or current business statistics, to influence your reading of the averages.

Average Up Rather Than Down

HAMILTON BELIEVED THAT it was much better to increase a line (i.e. one's holdings) on rising prices than to average down on falling prices, and the advice is worth remembering. No trader should buy a stock unless he believes it due for an advance. There are, of course, some men who buy stocks on a declining market to put away as permanent investments. No criticism is intended of that market operation.

The first thing a trader must learn is that his commitments should at all times be limited to an amount which he can, if fate decrees, afford to lose.

Hamilton often said that the majority of opinion in the Street was seldom right. Assuming him to have been correct, then the trader who understands the Dow Theory should not hesitate to put out a short line of stocks if the market action indicates to him that this would be a wise move, even though sentiment on Wall Street is overwhelmingly bullish. Many times when Wall Street was bullish Hamilton would remark that there was entirely too much company on the constructive side; at other times, when public opinion was extremely bearish, he would warn his readers that there was too much company on that side and that the Dow-Jones averages were saying that the market was perhaps oversold.

Seven Winners Out of Ten

THE QUESTION IS frequently asked, "What percentage of trades, timed in accordance with a reasonably competent interpretation of the Dow Theory, will be profitable?" It is the writer's belief that any trader endowed with ordinary market sense and plenty of patience who has studied and used the averages as a guide through the complete cycle of a bull and bear market should be able to make at least seven profitable turns out of every 10 efforts—and each profitable trade should net a gain in excess of the loss on a trade improperly timed. Many men have consistently bettered this record, but they seldom make more than four or five trades a year. They do not watch the tape but play for the important movements and are not concerned with a few points loss or gain.

The "Line" Formation

T HERE ARE PEOPLE who insist on trying to place an exact mathematical interpretation on the duration of a "line," but this cannot be done successfully. The allowable price variation must be considered in connection with the prevailing activity of speculation and be compared with the violence or lack of violence of preceding fluctuations. This is one of the reasons why the successful application of the Dow Theory to speculation must be considered both an art and a science. Anyone attempting an exact mathematical interpretation of the Dow Theory is placing himself on a parity with the surgeon who tried to remove an appendix by cutting two inches deep at a point 38 inches above the patient's instep, regardless of the age, sex, height, or contour of his patient.

Students were warned that a line in one average alone has no forecasting value when Hamilton wrote that ". . . all past experience of the average has shown that unless such a line is made simultaneously by both the industrials and the railroads it is more apt to be deceptive than not." (3/20/1916)

Don't "Always" Be in the Market

ANY PERSON WHO tries to be in the market at all times is almost certain to lose money, for there are many periods when even the most skillful trader is in doubt as to what will happen.

A wise man lets the market alone when the averages disagree.

Confirmation of the Averages

THE AUTHORITY OF new highs or lows which are properly confirmed remains in force until cancelled by some later definite confirmed action. If, for instance, new highs are made in a primary bull market the prediction is valid that the bull market will continue for a considerable time. Moreover, if one average later retraces its advance to a point below its old high, or even below a previous low point, but the other average fails to confirm the action, it is proper to infer that the previous bullish indication is still in force.

RICHARD
RUSSELL

Leading Present-Day Dow Theorist

During market crises or critical turning points the press associations and *Barron's* have often turned to Richard Russell for his interpretation of the stock market picture in terms of the Dow Theory. Although not alone in this field, Russell seems to have been thrown into the role of heir apparent to the Dow Theory sceptre.

Russell was born July 22, 1924 in New York City, where he was also educated. He began his market studies in the mid-1940's and began his market education the hard way, investing his own money.

At first, like most beginners in Wall Street, he had expensive lessons to learn. But over the years he bore down on his technical studies and has since fared well.

He began writing occasional articles in *Barron's*, starting in December, 1958, which is also around the period he began publishing his periodic "Dow Theory Letters."

Russell wrote one book, entitled "The Dow Theory Today" in 1960. More recently, he moved from New York to San Diego, California for the sake of his daughter's health, and still operates his service there.

The Wisdom of
RICHARD RUSSELL

Relative Strength

THE FIRST DISCUSSION of the use of relative strength (R.S.) techniques as an aid in stock selection appeared in *Barron's* in the issue of May 8, 1933. The article was written by Robert Rhea and was entitled "Stock Habits." In this article Rhea explained how he computed (during a given advance) the percentage of appreciation in the Industrial Average and the percentage of appreciation in a varied list of stocks. By comparing the **percentage of change** in each stock with the percentage of change in the Dow, Rhea was able to establish whether the stock was performing better or worse than the "market."

Furthermore, Rhea concluded that if a stock performed consistently better or worse than a market over a few swings, that relative strength or weakness was very likely to continue.

If we divide the price of a stock by the price of any convenient Average, we will obtain a ratio figure. If the stock (over a period of time) outperforms the Average, the ratio figure will rise; the converse is true if the stock performs worse than the Average. These two statistics (i.e. the price of the stock and the ratio figure) are then plotted on **semi-logarithmic** graph paper. One line of the graph will show the stock's actual movements in terms of percentages (since "log" paper deals in percentages), and the other line will show whether the stock is performing better or worse than the Average (and this too will be shown in percentages). This second line is the R.S. line, and conclusions drawn from the trend of R.S. can be extremely important in the selection of stocks.

I have noted that since 1959 each broad market movement seems to have been increasingly difficult from the technical standpoint. Stocks that "acted" beautifully during the 1953-56 and 1958-59 rises began (after 1959) to behave erratically, as far as technical analysis was concerned. I have little doubt that part of the difficulty stemmed from the astounding rise of technical analysis and charting throughout the nation. It seemed as if "too many cooks were spoiling the broth," and the more converts to charting, the more misleading the charts seemed to become. Finally, the 1961 "top" materialized into a classic of "false breakouts," erratic starts, and costly rises and reversals. After the 1962 collapse, the market started up with many stocks having failed to form any recognizable base of accumulation or, for that matter, any orthodox pattern at all. One simply had to buy them with the hope that they would continue to rise.

During the period since 1959 and particularly since 1961, I tested every conceivable method in a continuing search for a tool which might aid in stock selection. Technical analysis of individual stock charts were proving inadequate.

From my own experience, I believed that relative strength studies might be the answer. I know that R.S. trends were persistent, often lasting as long or considerably longer than a given movement in the general market. Furthermore, if the market was rising or simply moving sideways, and a stock was showing improving R.S., then obviously that stock was on its way up. **It did not matter whether the stock was break-**

ing out of a triangle or any other pattern, since improving R.S. in a static or rising market means appreciation.

From this, the following progression seemed logical: (1) **Start** with those stock groups which show the best R.S.—preferably groups which are in the act of definitely turning up after long R.S. declines. (2) Pick the stocks with the best R.S. within the strong R.S. groups. (3) Then pick the stocks with the best actual technical patterns from the strong R.S. stocks. These final choices can be expected to outperform during any market movement. But when they stop outperforming, when their R.S. line reverses or when the general market registers a "sell signal"— they should be sold.

The D.J. 30-Week Moving Average

THE RELATIONSHIP OF the Industrial Average to its own long-term (30-week) moving average is a meaningful one. During a major bull swing, Industrials tend to hold above their moving average (M.A.) and the opposite is true during a major decline. The manner in which the Industrial Average penetrates its own M.A. at the beginning of a move is also significant—and this whole relationship is worth studying.

Follow the Industrial Average and its M.A. (weekly) from early 1958 to the present. The 1958-59 rise traced a bullish pattern (with Industrials holding continuously above their M.A.) until 1959. In September, 1959, the senior Average turned down and penetrated its M.A. A few weeks later, Industrials embarked on a new rally above the M.A., but here we note that the M.A. was tending to "flatten out." A **second downward penetration** by Industrials through the M.A. occurred in January, 1960, and this proved to be the final bearish signal. The second penetration was followed by ten months of generally lower prices.

Another major rise began in October, 1960. The new

bull movement continued until January, 1962. In January, the Industrial Average turned down and penetrated its M.A. An attempt at a rally followed, but by February, 1962, the M.A. was seen to be moving sideways again. In March, the Industrial Average plunged below its M.A. for the **second time,** and this action was followed by the famous 1962 collapse.

The market struck bottom in June, 1962. A new bull movement took hold—then gathered momentum towards the end of the year. The rise continued until well into 1963. In July, 1963, Industrials turned down and violated their M.A. A rally started on July 24, and the first week of August saw the Industrial Average rise above its M.A. again.

Of interest is the fact that Industrials bettered their M.A. in April, 1958, and held above the M.A. until September, 1959—a period of **17 months.** Following the 1959-60 decline, Industrials pushed above their M.A. in December, 1960, and held above the M.A. until January, 1962—a period of **13 months.** Subsequent to the 1962 "crash," Industrials moved above the M.A. in October, 1962, and held above the M.A. until July, 1962—a period of **9 months.** Each of the swings since 1949 seems to have produced less upward force and less upward momentum.

D.J. Industrial Yields

OW AND HAMILTON always attached the utmost importance to values. "Stocks fluctuate together," wrote Dow, "but prices are controlled by values in the long run." Again he observed, "The tendency of prices over a considerable period of time will always be towards values."

A study of market history reveals that the cycles of stock values tend to extremes. At the bottom of the 1932, 1942, and 1949 bear markets, the average yield on the Dow-Jones industrials was 10.3%, 7.9% and 6.9% respectively. The bull market highs of 1929 put the average yield of the D-J industrials at 3.1%, 1937 at 3.7% and 1946 at 3.3%.

It is obvious, then, that bull markets have usually ended when values, as measured by the average yield on the D-J industrials, enter a zone of about 3.5% or less. In 1902 Dow wrote, "When a stock sells at a price which returns only 3½% on the investment, it is obviously dear, except there be some special reason for the established price. In the long run, the prices of stocks adjust themselves to the return on the investment, and while this is not a safe guide at all times, it is a guide that should never be laid aside or overlooked." Dow's words concerning stock values have proved amazingly accurate as a guide for the investor who buys and sells values.

Bull Peaks

THE DEGREE OF public participation and speculation have proved helpful gauges with which to measure the market. Here is Robert Rhea's description of the great 1929 top: "All the usual indications of inflation were present. Volume of trading was excessive and broker's loans were making new peaks regularly—in fact, call money rates were so high that many corporations were finding it profitable to liquidate inventories and lend their cash equivalent to Wall Street at fantastic returns. Pool activities were being conducted on a disgraceful scale, brokerage houses were hanging out S.R.O. signs, and leading stocks were yielding less than the best grade bonds.

"Worthless equities were being sky-rocketed without regard for intrinsic worth or earning power. The whole country appeared insane on the subject of stock speculation. Veteran traders look back at those months and wonder how they could have become so inculcated with the 'new era' view as to have been caught in the inevitable crash. Bankers whose good sense might have saved the situation had speculators listened to them, were shouted down as destructionists, while other bankers, whose names will go down in history as 'racketeers' were praised as supermen."

During such times, it is obvious that, regardless of the fact that the averages may be indicating the continuance of a bull market, the end cannot be far off. Most Dow Theorists would gladly sell out of a market which has all the earmarks of a third phase climax; they never wait for the actual bear signal. Often, on the advent of a bear signal, stocks drop so fast that it is impossible to obtain quotes on securities.

Dow Theory Is Technical, but Reveals Fundamentals

THE DOW THEORY is a completely technical approach to the market. It derives nothing from business statistics, indexes of production, economic reports, or any of the other thousands of facts that make up a study of the fundamental condition of the country. Operating on the principle that the averages take all these systems and much more into consideration, the Theory becomes a study of the movements of the averages themselves. The Dow Theorist believes that most of the fundamentalist's facts are already history. The market is not interested in yesterday or today; it is concerned only with tomorrow. It is the nature of the averages to contain all of the fundamentalist's facts plus the judgments and opinions of thousands of insiders, speculators, investors and businessmen, each viewing the market from the standpoint of his own business and general economy.

Hamilton illustrated this when he wrote, "The farmers say . . . 'what does Wall Street know about farming?' Wall Street knows more than all the farmers put together ever knew, with all that the farmers have forgotten. It can, moreover, refresh its memory instantly at any moment. It employs the ablest of the farmers, and its experts are better even than those of our admirable and little appreciated Department of Agriculture, whose publications Wall Street reads even if the farmer neglects them." Against this knowledge contained in the averages, says the Dow Theorist, the fundamentalist can seldom, if ever win.

Market Philosophy

BEFORE PURCHASING STOCKS for my own account, I ask myself the following questions. Are stocks great "values," and are leading investment-grade issues now providing historically attractive yields? Can I buy good stocks in a quiet market, stocks which offer hopes of appreciation over the years (with but little risk of decline because of high, well-covered dividends)? Is the prevailing opinion dead bearish in the face of a market that grows dull and refuses to decline? Obviously, these are **ideal** (or bear market bottom) conditions, and we can forget them for now.

In the absence of the above conditions, I ask myself the next series of questions: is this the bottom of a full correction in what I assume to be a continuing and technically strong bull market? Are stocks (or at least many stocks) still attractive values? Has the bull market progressed without showing any signs of a third phase "top"? Are most stocks in good basing patterns, and do they show signs of having been under strong accumulation? These conditions describe markets such as late 1953-early

1954 or late 1957-early 1958. We must also try a third series of criteria.

Is the advance still "strong" from the technical standpoint? Are the two Averages, Industrials and Rails, rising to successive confirmed highs? Is volume tending to rise with higher prices? Are the majority of stocks (as measured by the Advance-Decline ratio) confirming the rise by taking the A-D ratio to fresh new highs? Are daily new highs tending to expand as the Averages push higher? Do stocks rise, hold their gains relatively well, then push out again to new highs? Is there general skepticism regarding the rise, and are the odd-lotters selling in the face of the advance? Is the short interest ratio (a gauge of relative skepticism) holding above 1.5 and preferably above 1.75? Is the rise tending to "spread out" among the laggard and secondary issues or is it confined to a handful of strong stocks and a few strong groups? If these questions add up on the positive side, I am willing to call it a "good speculative market" and I am willing to commit a portion of my funds.

The Stock-Bond Yield Relationship

T HE YIELD DIFFERENTIAL between the D-J Industrials and Barron's 10 Highest-Grade Bonds measures
values.

Historically, common stocks have been priced to yield
more than fixed debt instruments or bonds. On infrequent
occasions, common stocks have yielded less than bonds,
but these areas have usually coincided with the formation
of important market tops. Consciously or unconsciously,
"big money" tends to move out of equities when the
yield on equities is less attractive than the yield on bonds.
The **"normal"** or historical stock-bond yield relationship
is therefore expressed by a positive (or plus) yield differential, a differential in favor of bonds.

This positive yield differential held in effect during most
of the 1940's (except for 1945-46) and most of the 1950's.
But in late-1958 the yield on the D-J Industrial Average
dropped below 4% and also below the yield on Barron's
10 Highest-Grade Bonds. Thus the stock-bond yield spread
turned **negative.**

The negative spread reached —1.6 in late-1959; at the

same time the average Industrial yield dropped to approximately 3%. These **extremes** in the stock-bond yield relationship and in stock yields proved too much for the market, and a major decline followed. This decline, which carried to the lows of 1960, did not correct the negative yield spread, but despite this a new market advance occurred. Toward late 1961 the Average Industrial yield dropped to 3.2% while the negative stock-bond yield spread widened to —1.5. Important distribution took place in that area, and the resultant collapse took Industrials below their 1960 low.

Nevertheless, at no time during 1962 did the negative-yield-spread reverse, and except for a few weeks in June the average Industrial yield remained in the 3.2 to 3.9% area. In mid-1962 another advance began. The 1963-64 advance again pushed the yield relationship to extremes. As of 3/1/64, the average yield on the D-J Industrials stood at 3.3% while the negative stock-bond yield differential was approximately —1.06. Thus average Industrial yields were back in the adverse 3 to 3.5% area, and the negative stock-bond yield returned to the very negative —1. to —2.% zone. Under these conditions it becomes difficult to talk about "investing" in equities, and it should be understood that the historical yield and stock-bond yield relationships put equities in the upper range of what must be considered an area of overvaluation.

New Highs and Lows

DURING A MAJOR bull movement, it is normal to see stock after stock push out of their established patterns and rise to new highs for the year. If the upward momentum continues, those stocks which recorded new highs will continue to rise, and they will be joined by fresh "breakouts" which will also augment the "new high parade."

But when a bull movement shows a steady decrease in the number of new highs, it is a sign that the original rallying strength is ebbing. Such a market, regardless of temporary rallies or confusing fluctuations, may be said to be "living on borrowed time." It is axiomatic that diminishing strength during a market advance will gradually turn into increasing weakness. By the same token, decreasing weakness during a market decline will materialize into a growing strength.

art II

isdom From The Big Boom Of...
... The Twenties

In the Twenties, the Great Operators and the Big Plungers were conspicuously active. At the same time, they were joined by increasing numbers of small investors, people from all walks of life, many of whom had never owned, let alone traded, common stocks before. The result was one of the great speculative eras in Wall Street. That it ended in grief does not detract from its heyday. While it was roaring along, the market of the Twenties was the most active, most exhilarating boom ever witnessed, and from it emerged a new market literature written by those attempting to understand its flights and to profit from them.

FREDERICK DREW BOND . .
Commentator of the Teens
and Twenties.

JESSE L. LIVERMORE . . The
Last of the Big Plungers.

WILLIAM D. GANN . . Advisor
to Traders of the Twenties.

FREDERICK DREW BOND

Wall Street Commentator of the Teens and Twenties

It's not altogether a pun to say that Bond was a "bonded writer" of Wall Street; i.e. he was guaranteed to do a good job by his background; he was a "newspaperman's newspaperman." His schooling was superb and his jobs led him to perfect order up the ladder, in precise and proper stages. He was correctly groomed for the role he was to play.

Born in Philadelphia on May 22, 1876, Frederick Drew Bond attended private schools, La Salle College and the University of Pennsylvania where he earned a B.S. degree.

In the business world he became first a newspaper reporter, then a copy reader, and finally a city editor. This was in Philadelphia and New York from 1899 to 1905.

Soon after, his interests turned exclusively to Wall Street, and by 1910 he was widely known as a financial consultant.

Bond became a prolific author on a wide range of financial subjects. His books include: *Stock Prices,* (published by Moody's Magazine, 1911, the forerunner of Moody's Investors Service); *The Need for Currency Reform,* 1911; *Stock Movements and Speculation,* 1928; *Success in Security Operations* (Copyright 1931 Chilton Books, Phila. and N.Y.); he also contributed financial articles to periodicals.

He died in 1951 at the age of 75.

The Wisdom of
FREDERICK D. BOND

Bull Market Factors

T O SAY THAT nothing affects stock prices save through the minds of buyers and sellers might seem a mere platitude, but as a matter of fact, it is common to hear a rise in the rate of interest, the defeat of a nation in war, an earthquake or some other notable event ascribed as a cause of stock movements; the seeming implication being often, that in some vague way these facts do, of themselves, make the prices. In a sense, indeed such statements, as well as the metaphor which speaks of the stock market as the "barometer of business" are convenient shorthand expressions, but, in another sense, they are not infrequently the token of a confusion of thought.

Stock prices may thus be regarded as the resultant of three general factors; there is, the psychological factor of hopes and fears of the participants conjoined with the capital which they are financially able to move. Secondly, there is the relation of the banks to the market, and this relation, as will be seen, not only limits in general the extent of price swings from the presumed investment point but it makes possible these speculative swings themselves by the extension and withdrawal of credit. Finally we have to consider the third factor, the manner in which, at a given time, the shares of a company are actually distributed and held in the market.

No more mischievous advice has ever been given than the counsel to make money in the stock market by selling when the public buy. There are a handful of alert bears who in a bull market are able to make money but they are exceptions. Professional and semi-professional speculators in a bull market are backing the same belief as the public speculator—namely, that prices will go higher. The essential difference between the professional bull and the amateur lies in how and when and what and how much each buys for the rise.

Since the public are always willing to buy when they think prices will go higher, a bull market terminates when, and only when, the public have no more funds with which to take on additional stock; or to put the matter from a slightly different angle, when public bids at a given price level are less than the combined offerings of stock by previous speculative holders, syndicate and investors who have decided to sell out.

This fact leads to the observation that thoughtful and well-informed speculators sometimes seriously under-estimate the duration of a bull market. By the time the market is half-way up, this class concludes with entire correctness that prices are too high when judged from an investment standpoint; hence, they believe that the bull market is near its termination. The basic error in this reasoning is due to lack of recognition of the acquisitive motives and intentions which are the propelling causes behind a bull market. The error here lies in forming a judgment of speculative movement on a basis of investment conditions. It is true that investment and banking conditions ultimately limit the great swings of the market both up and down; but within these widely extended swings it is, in general, speculative factors which cause the price movements.

Bears Can Never Be Out of Touch

TURNING TO THE question of operations in a bear market, the first thing which invites notice is that the speculator must be in constant and immediate touch with the market and with his broker.

This is partly due to the fact that the market may move both abruptly and quickly, but it is also due to the fact that a bear can rely fully on no one else for information. Brokerage firms, and especially the managers of customers' rooms, are inveterately bullish, with extremely few exceptions. To await information from men in this frame of mind may cause a bear to miss good opportunities of selling short, may cause him to be caught in a sudden rally, or to miss the bottom of the decline. This means that the bear must either take up speculation as his profession, or must, at least, be entirely free from confinement to any other business calling. There are few things more bitter than to foresee correctly the course of a great break and yet make out of it little or nothing.

Traders Follow Trends, They Do Not Make Them

A S CUSTOMERS ASSEMBLE to watch the ticker it is on the current fluctuations of the market that their commitments are based. Whether they discern its immediate course correctly or not, all traders can always see one thing—whether the market is advancing or declining. It is on this single unequivocal fact that the great majority of the commitments in customers' rooms are made. The longer the market keeps going up and, consequently, the nearer it must be to its top, the more speculators—the more of the "public"—enter on the scene and buy shares, attracted by the great activity and by stories of gains and all hoping for still higher and higher prices. Thus whether successful or not, the great mass of commission house traders who attempt to discern the coming trend of the market simply from what it is doing at the moment, do not make the current trend themselves. They follow it. It is true that by this trailing behind the market, an ever growing mass of speculators have, at rather rare intervals, become responsible by their combined buying for a rise of prices to heights which, otherwise, they could not have touched. An instance of this sort of thing was in April 1901, though, even here, their uniform, if incoherent, action was sustained and directed by the concerted activity of wealthy individuals and interests concerned in the course of prices. But in any event, no matter how the speculative "public" may enhance and protract the trend of the market, they **follow** it as it presents itself to them; they do not **make** it.

But if the public do not make the trend of the market, neither do the few hundred room traders on the Exchange floor, whose commitments are usually cleaned up overnight. Of course, individuals among them may anticipate the course of prices and by acting on this anticipation help to create it. Moreover, it is true that this picked body of speculators discern the signs of the day-to-day trend earlier and far better than the average commission house customer; but generally speaking, the fact that room traders are usually thus alert to seize the course of prices is, in itself, a statement that though they may reinforce this course, they do not make it.

JESSE L. LIVERMORE

The Last of the Big Plungers

One of the most colorful of the legendary speculators in Wall Street history, Jesse L. Livermore, was born in West Acton, Massachusetts, in 1877. He started work as a marking boy, chalking up prices on the board for Paine Webber, and began to speculate with the first few dollars he earned. By the age of 15 Livermore had made $1,000 in the stock market. He also completed four years of mathematics in one year while holding down his job at the brokerage house.

He continued his all-or-nothing type of manoeuvring and made a fortune while still a boy. On Wall Street he was called "The Boy Plunger" and the name stuck for the rest of his picturesque life. His first killing was made selling short.

Eventually, Livermore became a big-time operator, with his own private boardroom and 30 direct-to-broker telephones, and he spread his action among all of them. When he was a bear trader after the 1929 crash he had a bodyguard, for bears were (and still are) unpopular.

He went bankrupt four times, but bounded back each time. His market philosophy is contained in a single book authored by Livermore, "How to Trade in Stocks" published by Duell, Sloan & Pearce early in 1940, reprinted with permission of Duell, Sloan & Pearce, Inc. by Investors Press Inc.

Apparently in a state of melancholy, he shot himself in

the cloakroom of the Sherry Netherlands Hotel, 5th Avenue at 59th, New York, on November 28th, 1940. He died the next day, at the age of 63. It was front page news in the New York *Times,* even though it was more than a decade since Livermore had been a daily byword on Wall Street, for Livermore had been one of the biggest of the big guns in the famous bull market leading up to 1929 and the infamous bear market which followed.

Although often called the "Bear of Bears" Livermore claims to have made more money, and more easily, as a bull than a bear. And ironically, many give him a large part of the credit for starting the long bull market which preceded the 1929 crash. He had a private telegraph operator presiding over a system of private wires, and played both the long and short side of the market. A squad of expert statisticians waded daily through mountains of data and libraries of books in order to keep the boss informed on the outside world.

But although he was often a bear, especially during the 1929-1932 crash, there never was any evidence that he ever headed any bear raids or worked with others to drive a price down. He was content to **ride** a stock down, rather than **force** it down.

Livermore could speak from strength, for he was a speculator for an entire generation. After the 1907 panic he walked out of the wreckage of Wall Street with $3,000,000.

Though bankrupt and owing $4,000,000 in 1915, he borrowed more capital, speculated on the bull side in Bethlehem and U.S. Steel and by 1917 had made enough to pay off his creditors and buy $1,000,000 in Liberty Bonds.

He also correctly predicted the vigorous 1921 and 1927 market advances. In 1929 he felt the market was overvalued but finally threw in the sponge (and became bullish), much too prematurely, in November. But he quickly cut his losses and switched to the short side.

Livermore listed two major points for success:
1. Sensitiveness to mob psychology.
2. Willingness to take a loss.

He chain-smoked cigars, wore dark suits and drove gaily colored Rolls Royces, preferably dazzling yellow. He was ever-willing to venture his entire fortune in one transaction.

It is reputed that Livermore had no regular brokerage accounts but called or dropped into this brokerage house and that, leaving orders to buy or sell. He would sell 5,000 shares of a stock one day in a Palm Beach branch office and buy the next morning in Miami, baffling those who tried to follow his movements.

By 1929 Livermore was just about the only "pure" titanic speculator left. Most of the other legendary names of that year were giants of industry **first** and giants of Wall Street **second.** Also, by 1929 the stock market had grown too large for "raids" to be truly successful.

He was almost always both long and short in the stock market at the same time. It was his practice not to get into any stock positions that could not be sold in 15 minutes. This implies he limited the size of his positions to what could be readily sold without a large price sacrifice, and that he usually traded in large or popular issues. The 15-minute principle was sacrosanct.

Additionally, it is interesting to note he usually bought and sold "at the market," not at fixed prices.

Livermore has left his mark on the Street as few others have done before or since; old-timers remember him as the most daring speculator of the century.

The Wisdom of
JESSE L. LIVERMORE

Take Small Losses

PROFITS ALWAYS TAKE care of themselves, but losses never do. The speculator has to insure himself against considerable losses by taking **the first small loss.** In doing so he keeps his account in order, so that at some future time, when he has a constructive idea, he will be in a position to go into another deal, taking on the same amount of stock as he had when he was wrong.

Uptrend Patterns

IT MAY SURPRISE many to know that in my method of trading, when I see by my records that an upward trend is in progress I become a buyer as soon as a stock makes a new high on its movement, after having a normal reaction. The same applies whenever I take the short side. Why? Because I am following the trend at the time. My records signal me to go ahead!

I never buy on reactions or go short on rallies . . . Never average losses. Let that thought be written indelibly upon your mind.

At the beginning of the move you will notice a very large volume of sales with gradually advancing prices for a few days. Then what I term a "Normal Reaction" will occur. On that reaction the sales volume will be much less than on the previous days of its advance . . .

In a day or two activity will start again, and the volume will increase. If it is a real movement, in a short space of time the natural, normal reaction will have been recovered, and the stock will be selling in new high territory. That movement should continue strong for a few days with only minor daily reactions. Sooner or later it will reach a point where it is due for another normal reaction. When it occurs, it should be on the same lines as the first reaction, because that is the natural way any stock will act when it is in a definite trend.

At the first part of a movement of this kind the distance above the previous high point to the next high point is not very great. But as time goes on you will notice that it is making much faster headway on the upside . . .

When it resumes its advance again in a few days, you will notice that the volume of sales at that time is not nearly as large as it was at the beginning of the move. The stock is becoming harder to buy. That being the case, the next points in the movement will be much more rapid than before.

Don't Trade Every Day

THERE ARE ONLY a few times a year, possibly four or five, when you should allow yourself to make any commitment at all. In the interims you are letting the market shape itself for the next big movement.

If you have timed the movement correctly, your first commitment will show you a profit at the start. From then on, all that is required of you is to be alert, watching for the appearance of the danger signal to tell you to step aside and convert paper profits into real money.

Remember this: When you are doing nothing, those speculators who feel they must trade day in and day out, are laying the foundation for your next venture. You will reap benefits from their mistakes.

Most people are so engrossed with the minor ups and downs that they miss the big movements.

Some Livermore "Pearls of Wisdom"

A GAMBLER IS A man who doesn't know the market. He goes to a broker and says "What can I do to make a thousand dollars?" He is only an incident. The speculative investor buys or sells against future conditions on his knowledge of what has happened in the past under a similar set of conditions.

From my viewpoint the investors are the big gamblers. They make a bet, stay with it, and if all goes wrong, they lose it all. . . .

Do not have an interest in too many stocks at one time. It is much easier to watch a few than many. . . .

I know but one sure tip from a broker. It is your margin call. When it reaches you, close your account. You are on the wrong side of the market.

One major mistake of all speculators is the urge to enrich themselves in too short a time. Instead of taking two or three years to make 500% on their capital, they try to do it in two or three months.

A speculator should make it a rule each time he closes out a successful deal to take one-half of his profits and lock this sum up in a safe deposit box. The only money that is ever taken out of Wall Street by speculators is the money they draw out of their accounts after closing a successful deal. . . .

Stock market intuition is like that of a bridge player. After a man has played bridge all his life he knows when to finesse instinctively.

Stay With a Winner

EXPERIENCE HAS PROVED to me that the real money made in speculating has been in commitments in a stock or commodity showing a profit right from the start.

You immediately become fearful that if you don't take the profit the next day you may see it fade away—so out you go with a small profit, when that is the very time you should entertain all the hope in the world. Why should you worry about losing two points' profit which you did not have the previous day?

If you can make two points' profit in one day, you might take two or three the next, and perhaps five more the next week. As long as the stock is acting right, and the market is right, do not be in a hurry to take a profit. You know you are right, because if you were not, you would have no profit at all. Let it ride and ride along with it. It may grow into a very large profit, and as long as the action of the market does not give you any cause to worry, have the courage of your convictions and stay with it.

Wait for the Breakout

IN A NARROW market when the prices are not getting anywhere to speak of, but move within a narrow range, there is no sense in trying to anticipate the next big movement, whether it is going to be up or down. The thing to do is watch the market to determine the limits of the get-nowhere prices and make up your mind that you will not take an interest until prices break through the limits in either direction.

WILLIAM D. GANN

Adviser to Traders of the Twenties

William D. Gann, born and educated in Texas, arrived in New York in 1903, working as a registered representative, a stock market letter writer, and an analyst until 1919.

In that year, Gann launched forth with his own advisory organization publishing a market letter called "Supply and Demand."

He is remembered chiefly because of eight books for investors, widely known in their day.

The best known were *Wall Street Stock* Selector (Financial Guardian Publishing Co., 1930); *45 Years in Wall Street* (Lambert Gann Publishing Co., 1949); and *Truth of the Stock Tape* (Financial Guardian Publishing Co., 1923).

Gann died June 14, 1955, at the age of 77.

The Wisdom of
WILLIAM D. GANN

Twenty-four Rules for Traders

IN ORDER TO make a success trading in the stock market, the trader must have definite rules and follow them. The rules given below are based upon my personal experience and anyone who follows them will make a success.

1. Amount of capital to use: Divide your capital into 10 equal parts and never risk more than one-tenth of your capital on any one trade.

2. Use stop loss orders. Always protect a trade when you make it, with a stop loss order 3 to 5 points away.

3. Never overtrade. This would be violating your capital rule.

4. Never let a profit run into a loss. After you once have a profit of 3 points or more, raise your stop loss order so that you will have no loss of capital.

5. Do not buck the trend. Never buy or sell if you are not sure of the trend according to your charts.

6. When in doubt, get out, and don't get in when in doubt.

7. Trade only in active stocks. Keep out of slow, dead ones.

8. Equal distribution of risk. Trade in 4 or 5 stocks, if possible. Avoid tying up all your capital in any one stock.
9. Never limit your orders or fix a buying or selling price. Trade at the market.
10. Don't close your trades without good reason. Follow up with a stop loss order to protect your profits.
11. Accumulate a surplus. After you have made a series of successful trades, put some money into surplus account to be used only in emergency or in times of panic.
12. Never buy just to get a dividend.
13. Never average a loss. This is one of the worst mistakes a trader can make.
14. Never get out of the market just because you have lost patience or get into the market because you are tired of waiting.
15. Avoid taking small profits and big losses.
16. Never cancel a stop loss order after you have placed it at the time you make a trade.
17. Avoid getting in and out of the market too often.
18. Be just as willing to sell short as you are to buy. Let your object be to keep with the trend and make money.
19. Never buy just because the price of a stock is low or sell short just because the price is high.
20. Be careful about pyramiding at the wrong time. Wait until the stock is very active and has crossed Resistance Levels before buying more and until it has broken out of the zone of distribution before selling more.
21. Select the stocks with small volume of shares outstanding to pyramid on the buying side and the ones with the largest volume of stock outstanding to sell short.
22. Never hedge. If you are long of one stock and it starts to go down, do not sell another stock short to hedge it. Get out at the market; take your loss and wait for another opportunity.

23. Never change your position in the market without a good reason. When you make a trade, let it be for some good reason or according to some definite plan; then do not get out without a definite indication of a change in trend.
24. Avoid increasing your trading after a long period of success or a period of profitable trades.

"Targets" - A Bad Practice

THE MAJORITY OF people have a habit when they buy or sell a stock, of fixing in their minds a certain figure at which they expect to take profits. There is no reason or cause for this. It is simply a bad habit based on hope. When you make a trade, your object should be to make profits and there is no way that you can determine in advance how much profit you can expect on any one particular trade. The market itself determines the amount of your profit, and the thing that you must do is to be ready to get out and accept a profit whenever the trend changes, and not before.

Part III

Learning From 1929...

At first, it was still possible to believe that 1929 was only a "healthy" shake-out. And prices did rally in early 1930. But then they turned down decisively, and the great reappraisal began. One of the basic assumptions of the Cult of Common Stocks was that stock prices always did better, over time, than other traditional investments. But the seemingly endless depression of stock prices in the early Thirties began to raise some doubts, and there was a flood of investment writing trying to explain what had gone wrong and "what to do now."

JOHN K. GALBRAITH . . Historian of MARKET PANICS

BERNARD M. BARUCH . . Wall Street Elder Statesman

GLENN G. MUNN . . Bear Market Technician

JOHN K.
GALBRAITH

Historian of Market Panics

It fell upon a noted contemporary economist and author, John Kenneth Galbraith, to supply the first comprehensive view of 1929 in perspective, to thoroughly research the real reasons behind the spectacular fall in prices. Galbraith has summed up his studies in his classic work *The Great Crash* (published by Houghton Mifflin, 1955).

John Galbraith is many things: economist, diplomat, government administrator, writer, university professor.

Interspersed with teaching were appointments as an economic advisor to the National Defense Advisory Commission 1940-41; assistant administrator in charge of Price Division, Office of Price Administration, 1941-42; Directing Officer of Economic Security Policy, State Department, 1946, etc.

Few writers in the fields of economics and the stock market have enjoyed greater success on so broad a scale as Galbraith. His books include: *American Capitalism*, 1951; *A Theory of Price Control*, 1952; *The Great Crash* (Houghton Mifflin, Publishers), 1955; *The Affluent Society*, 1958; *The Liberal Hour*, 1960. His career has been full of such varied jobs, as those listed above, and also included membership on the Board of Editors of Fortune Magazine, from 1943-48. He lectured at Harvard in 1948-49 where he has been Professor of Economics since 1949, although he has been on special leave from Harvard for such tasks as American Ambassador to India in the Kennedy administration, with extraordinary assignments.

The quotations here are selected from *The Great Crash*, with its vivid portrayal of one of Wall Street's blackest periods.

The Wisdom of
JOHN K. GALBRAITH

Things Become More Serious

(Story Of the 1929 Panic)

IN THE AUTUMN of 1929 the New York Stock Exchange, under roughly its present constitution, was 112 years old. During this lifetime it had seen some difficult days. On September 18, 1873, the firm of Jay Cooke and Company failed, and, as a more or less direct result, so did fifty-seven other Stock Exchange firms in the next few weeks. On October 23, 1907, call money rates reached 125 per cent in the panic of that year. On September 16, 1920—the autumn months are the off-season in Wall Street—a bomb exploded in front of Morgan's next door, killing thirty people and injuring a hundred more.

A common feature of all these earlier troubles was that, having happened, they are over. The worst was reasonably recognizable as such. The singular feature of the great crash of 1929 was that the worst continued to worsen. What looked one day like the end proved on the next day to have been only the beginning. Nothing could have been more ingeniously designed to maximize the suffering, and also to insure that as few as possible escaped the common misfortune. The fortunate speculator who had funds to answer the first margin call presently got another and equally urgent one, and if he met that there would still be another. In the end all the money he had was extracted from him and lost. The man with the smart money, who was safely out of the market when the first crash came, naturally went back in to pick up bargains. (Not only were a recorded 12,894,650 shares sold on October 24; precisely the same number were bought.) The bargains then suffered a ruinous fall. Even the man who waited out all of October and all of November, who saw the volume of trading return to normal and saw Wall Street become as placid as a product market, and who then bought common stocks would see their value drop to a third or a fourth of the purchase price in the next twenty-four months. The Coolidge bull market was a remarkable phenomenon. The ruthlessness of its liquidation was, in its own way, equally remarkable.

II

Monday, October 28, was the first day on which this process of climax and anticlimax **ad infinitum** began to reveal itself. It was another terrible day. Volume was huge, although below the previous Thursday—nine and a quarter million shares as compared with nearly thirteen. But the losses were far more severe. The *Times* industrials were down 49 points for the day. General Electric was off 48; Westinghouse, 34; Tel and Tel, 34. Steel went down 18 points. Indeed, the decline on this one day was greater than that of all the preceding week of panic. Once again a late ticker left everyone in ignorance of what was happening, save that it was bad.

On this day there was no recovery. At one-ten Charles E. Mitchell was observed going into Morgan's, and the news ticker carried the magic word. Steel rallied and went from 194 to 198. But Richard Whitney did not materialize. It seems probable in light of later knowledge that Mitchell was on the way to float a personal loan. The market weakened again, and in the last hour a phenomenal three million shares

147

—a big day's business before and ever since—changed hands at rapidly falling prices.

At four-thirty in the afternoon the bankers assembled once more at Morgan's, and they remained in session until six-thirty. They were described as taking a philosophical attitude, and they told the press that the situation "retained hopeful features," although these were not specified. But the statement they released after the meeting made clear what had been discussed for the two hours. It was no part of the bankers' purpose, the statement said, to maintain any particular level of prices or to protect anyone's profit. Rather the aim was to have an orderly market, one in which offers would be met by bids at some price. The bankers were only concerned that "air holes," as Mr. Lamont dubbed them, did not appear.

Like many lesser men, Mr. Lamont and his colleagues had suddenly found themselves overcommitted on a falling market. The time had come to short on premises. Support, organized or otherwise, could not contend with the overwhelming, pathological desire to sell. The meeting had considered how to liquidate the commitment to support the market without adding to the public perturbation.

The formula that was found was a chilling one. On Thursday, Whitney had supported prices and protected profits—or stopped losses. This was what the people wanted. To the man who held stock on margin, disaster had only one face and that was falling prices. But now prices were to be allowed to fall. The speculator's only comfort, henceforth, was that his ruin would be accomplished in an orderly and becoming manner.

There were no recriminations at the time. Our political life favors the extremes of speech; the man who is gifted in the arts of abuse is bound to be a notable, if not always a great figure. In business, things are different. Here we are surprisingly gentle and forbearing. Even preposterous claims or excuses are normally taken, at least for all public purposes, at the face value. On the evening of the 28th no one any longer could feel "secure in the knowledge that the most powerful banks stood ready to prevent a recurrence" of panic. The market had reasserted itself as an impersonal force beyond the power of any person to control, and, while this is the way markets are supposed to be, it was horrible. But no one assailed the bankers for letting the people down. There was even some talk that on the next day the market might receive organized support.

III

Tuesday, October 29, was the most devastating day in the history of the New York stock market, and it may have been the most devastating day in the history of markets. It combined all of the bad features of all of the bad days before. Volume was immensely greater than on Black Thursday; the drop in prices was almost as great as on Monday. Uncertainty and alarm were as great as on either.

Selling began as soon as the market opened and in huge volume. Great blocks of stock were offered for what they would bring; in the first half-hour sales were at a 33,000,000 a-day rate. The air holes, which the bankers were to close, opened wide. Repeatedly and in many issues there was a plethora of selling orders and no buyers at all. The stock of White Sewing Machine Company, which had reached a high of 48 in the months preceding, had closed at 11 the night before. During the day someone—according to Frederick Lewis Allen it was thought to have been a bright messenger boy for the Exchange—had the happy idea of entering a bid for a block of stock at a dollar a share. In the absence of any other bid he got it. Once again, of course, the ticker lagged—at the close it was two and a half hours behind. By then, 16,410,030 sales had been recorded on the New York Stock Exchange —some certainly went unrecorded—or more than three times the number that was once considered a fabulously big day. (Only on the best days during the 1954 boom did volume go above three million.) The *Times* industrial averages were down 43 points, cancelling all of the gains of the twelve wonderful months preceding.

The losses would have been worse had there not been a closing rally. Thus Steel, for which Whitney had bid 205 on Thursday, reached 167 during the course of the day, although it rallied to 174 at the close. American Can opened at 130, dropped to 110, and rose to 120. Westinghouse opened at 131—on September 3 it had closed at 286—and dropped to 100. Then it rallied to 126. But the worst thing that happened on this terrible day was to the investment trusts. Not only did they go down, but it became apparent that they could go practically to nothing. Goldman Sachs Trading Corporation had closed at 60 the night before. During the day it dropped to 35 and closed at that level, off by not far short of half. Blue Ridge, its offspring once removed, on which the magic of leverage was now working in reverse, did much worse. Early in September it had sold at 24. By October 24 it was down to 12, but it resisted rather well the misfortunes of that day and the day following. On the morning of October 29 it opened at 10 and promptly slipped to 3, giving up more than two-thirds of its value. It recovered later but other investment trusts did less well; their stock couldn't be sold at all.

The worst day on Wall Street came eventually to an end. Once again the lights blazed all night. Members of the Exchange, their employees, and the employees of the Stock Exchange by now were reaching the breaking point from strain and fatigue. In this condition they faced the task of recording and handling the greatest volume of transactions ever. All of this was without the previous certainty that things might get better. They might go on getting worse. In one house an employee fainted from exhaustion, was revived, and put back to work again.

IV

In the first week the slaughter had been of the innocents. During this second week there is some evidence that it was the well-to-do and the wealthy who were being subjected to a leveling process comparable in magnitude and suddenness to that presided over a decade before by Lenin. The size of the blocks of stock which were offered suggested that big speculators were selling or being sold. Another indication came from the boardrooms. A week before they were crowded, now they were nearly empty. Those now in trouble had facilities for suffering in private.

The bankers met twice on the 29th—at noon and again in the evening. There was no suggestion that they were philosophical. This was hardly remarkable because, during the day, an appalling rumor had swept the Exchange. It was that the bankers' pool, so far from stabilizing the market, was actually selling stocks! The prestige of the bankers had in truth been falling even more rapidly than the market. After the evening session, Mr. Lamont met the press with the disenchanting task of denying that they had been liquidating securities—or participating in a bear raid. After explaining again, somewhat redundantly in view of the day's events, that it was not the purpose of the bankers to maintain a particular level of prices, he concluded: "The group has continued and will continue in a co-operative way to support the market and has not been a seller of stocks." In fact, as later intelligence revealed, Albert H. Wiggin of the Chase was personally short at the time to the tune of some millions. His co-operative support, which if successful would have cost him heavily, must have had an interesting element of ambivalence.

So ended the organized support. The phrase recurred during the next few days, but no one again saw in it any ground for hope. Few men ever lost position so rapidly as did the New York bankers in the five days from October 24 to October 29. The crash on October 24 was the signal for corporations and out-of-town banks, which had been luxuriating in the 10 per cent and more rate of interest, to recall their money from Wall Street. Between October 23 and October 30, as values fell and margin accounts were liquidated, the volume of brokers' loans fell by over a billion. But the corporations and the out-of-town banks responded to the horrifying news from New York—although, in fact, their funds were never seriously endangered—by calling home over two billions. The New York banks stepped into the gaping hole that was left by these summer financiers, and during that first week of crisis they increased their loans by about a billion. This was a bold step. Had the New York banks succumbed to the general fright, a money panic would have been added to the other woes. Stocks would have been dumped because their owners could not have borrowed money at any price to carry them. To prevent this was a considerable achievement for which all who owned stocks should have been thankful. But the banks received no credit. People remembered only that they had bravely undertaken to stem the price collapse and had failed.

Despite a flattering supposition to the contrary, people come readily to terms with power. There is little reason to think that the power of the great bankers, while they were assumed to have it, was much resented. But as the ghosts of numerous tyrants, from Julius Caesar to Benito Mussolini, will testify, people are very hard on those who, having had power, lose it or are destroyed. Then anger at past arrogance is joined with contempt for present weakness. The victim or his corpse is made to suffer all available indignities.

Such was the fate of the bankers. For the next decade they were fair game for congressional committees, courts, the press and the comedians. The great pretensions and the great failures of these days were a cause. A banker need not be popular; indeed, a good banker in a healthy capitalist society should probably be much disliked. People do not wish to trust their money to a hail-fellow-well-met but to a misanthrope who can say no. However, a banker must not seem futile, ineffective, or vaguely foolish. In contrast with the stern power of Morgan in 1907, that was precisely how his successors seemed, or were made to seem, in 1929.

The failure of the bankers did not leave the community entirely without constructive leadership. There was Mayor James J. Walker. Appearing before a meeting of motion picture exhibitors on that Tuesday, he appealed to them to "show pictures which will reinstate courage and hope in the hearts of the people."

V

On the Exchange itself, there was a strong feeling that courage and hope might best be restored by just closing up for a while. This feeling had, in fact, been gaining force for several days. Now it derived support from the simple circumstance that everyone was badly in need of sleep. Employees of some Stock Exchange firms had not been home for days. Hotel rooms in downtown New York were at a premium, and restaurants in the financial area had gone on to a fifteen and twenty-hour day. Nerves were bad, and mistakes were becoming increasingly common. After the close of trading on Tuesday, a broker found a large waste basket of unexecuted orders which he had set aside for early attention and had totally forgotten. One customer, whose margin account was impaired, was sold out twice. A number of firms needed some time to see if they were still solvent. There were, in fact, no important failures by Stock Exchange firms during these days, although one firm had reported itself bankrupt as the result of a clerical error by an employee who was in the last stages of fatigue.

Yet to close the Exchange was a serious matter. It might somehow signify that stocks had lost all their value, with consequences no one could foresee. In any case, securities would immediately become a badly frozen asset. This would be hard on wholly solvent investors who might need to realize on them or use them as collateral. And sooner or later a new "gutter" market would develop in which individuals would informally dispose of stocks to those increasingly exceptional individuals who still wanted to buy them.

In 1929 the New York Stock Exchange was in principle a sovereignty of its members. Apart from the general statutes relating to the conduct of business and the prevention of fraud, it was subject to no important state or federal regulation. This meant a considerable exercise of self-government. Legislation governing the conduct of trading had to be kept under review and enforced. Stocks had to be approved for listing. The building and other facilities of the Exchange had to be managed. As with the United States Congress, most of this work was done in committees. (These, in turn, were dominated by a somewhat smaller group of members who were expected and accustomed to run things.) A decision to close the Exchange had to be taken by the Governing Committee, a body of about forty members. The mere knowledge that this body was meeting would almost certainly have an unfavorable effect on the market.

Nonetheless, at noon on Tuesday, the 29th, a meeting was held. The members of the committee left the floor in twos and threes and went, not to the regular meeting room, but to the office of the President of the Stock Clearing Corporation directly below the trading floor. Some months later, Acting President Whitney described the session with considerable graphic talent. "The office they met in was never designed for large meetings of this sort, with the result that most of the Governors were compelled to stand, or to sit on tables. As the meeting proceeded, panic was raging overhead on the floor. Every few minutes the latest prices were announced, with quotations moving swiftly and irresistibly downwards. The feeling of those present was revealed by their habit of continually lighting cigarettes, taking a puff or two, putting them out and lighting new ones—a practice which soon made the narrow room blue with smoke and extremely stuffy."

The result of these nervous deliberations was a decision to meet again in the evening. By evening the late rally had occurred and it was decided to stay open for another day. The next day a further formula was hit upon. The Exchange would stay open. But it would have some special holidays and then go on short hours and this would be announced just as soon as the market seemed strong enough to stand it.

Many still wanted to close. Whitney said later, although no doubt with some exaggeration, that in the days to come, "the authorities of the Exchange led the life of hunted things, until (eventually) the desirability of holding the market open became apparent to all."

VI

The next day those forces were at work which on occasion bring

ress in the stock market and, like all booms, it had to end. On the first of January 1929, it was a simple matter of probability.

The position of the people who had at least a nominal responsibility for what was going on was a complex one. One of the oldest puzzles -of politics is who is to regulate the regulators. But an equally baffling problem, which has never received the attention it deserves, is who is to make wise those who are required to have wisdom.

A bubble can easily be punctured. But to incise it with a needle so that it subsides gradually is a task of no small delicacy. Among those who sensed what was happening in early 1929, there was some hope but no confidence that the boom could be made to subside. The real choice was between an immediate and deliberately engineered collapse and a more serious disaster later on. Someone would certainly be blamed for the ultimate collapse when it came. There was no question whatever as to who would be blamed should the boom be deliberately deflated. (For nearly a decade the Federal Reserve authorities had been denying their responsibility for the deflation of 1920-21.) The eventual disaster also had the inestimable advantage of allowing a few more days, weeks, or months of life. One may doubt if at any time in early 1929 the problem was ever framed in terms of quite such stark alternatives. But however disguised or evaded, these were the choices which haunted every serious conference on what to do about the market.

President Coolidge neither knew nor cared what was going on. A few days before leaving office in 1929, he cheerily observed that things were "absolutely sound" and that stocks were "cheap at current prices."

Now, as throughout history, financial capacity and political perspicacity are inversely correlated. Long-run salvation by men of business has never been highly regarded if it means disturbance in the present. So inaction will be advocated in the present even though it means deep trouble in the future. Here, at least equally with communism, lies the threat to capitalism. It is what causes men who know that things are going quite wrong to say that things are fundamentally sound.

BERNARD M. BARUCH

Wall Street's Elder Statesman

Bernard Baruch had strong opinions about what went wrong in 1929, which, as the country's elder statesman-financier, he has recounted to several U.S. presidents, along with many other matters.

Baruch was born August 19, 1870 in Camden, South Carolina, a second child of four. He was first educated in a private school but when his family moved to New York in 1881 he was sent to a public school, and later entered the College of the City of New York. His first job was in a firm of dealers in druggist's supplies, where he earned $3 a week.

He began his financial life in 1890, speculating on his own. In 1891 he joined the brokerage firm of A. A. Housman & Co., as a bond salesman and a customer's man. At the beginning of his career, Baruch, like Jesse Livermore, was engaged in "scalping" in the market, i.e. trading in and out for small quick profits. In 1896, at 26, he became a partner in A. A. Housman & Co., at which point Baruch began to emerge as a factor in Wall Street. Three years later he bought a seat on the New York Stock Exchange and became a large market operator.

By 1912, Baruch had become a millionaire, a major name in financial circles and, at 42, was ready to retire from brokerage duties, in order to concentrate on private speculation. In 1916 he was appointed a member of the Advisory Committee for the Council of National Defense, and in 1918 he became chairman of the War Industries Board. This was followed by a series of presidential appointments during World Wars I and II and at the United Nations thereafter.

Even after his retirement from Wall Street, Baruch's opinions on economic and stock matters were continually sought. He wrote for and was interviewed by scores of magazines, and he authored the book *My Own Story* © copyright 1957. Reprinted by permission of Holt, Rinehart & Winston, Inc. in which his colorful career is graphically described.

The Wisdom of
BERNARD M. BARUCH

Madness of the Crowd

I THINK THAT the depression of 1929 was due more to a world madness and delusion than anything else. It was somewhat similar to the Tulip Craze, the Mississippi Bubble, and the South Sea Bubble. The world seems to go mad at times, and has extraordinary delusions or crowd madness—as against witches. Or it may take the form of war. The Crusades were such a madness. Or it may take the form, and generally does in modern times, of great speculative madnesses. I think much of the legislation to prevent incompetency and corrupt practices in the sale of securities and regulation of the exchanges is good. The laws ought to be strengthened that will protect the public when they are in these periods of madness such as 1929 and the Florida Boom. That is going to be a difficult thing. But the world has been struck with those things over and over again. Whenever it finds itself in that mess, it turns around to look for an alibi for its own weakness, and its own mistakes. (I made some myself.) Then it also looks for a catharsis.

Whatever men attempt they seem driven to try to overdo.

Some Baruch Trading Philosophy

I N THE STOCK market the first loss is usually the small-
est. One of the worst mistakes anyone can make is to
hold on blindly and refuse to admit that his judgment
had been wrong.

Many a novice will sell something he has a profit in to
protect something in which he has a loss. Since the good
stock usually has gone down least, or may even show a
profit it is psychologically easy to let go. With a bad stock
the loss is likely to be very heavy and the impulse is to
hold on to it in order to recover what has been lost.

Actually, the procedure one should follow is to sell the
bad stock and keep the good stock. With rare exceptions,
stocks are high because they are good, and stocks are low
because they are of doubtful value.

Occasionally one is **too** close to a stock. In such cases
the more one knows about a subject—the more inside
information one has—the more likely one is to believe
that he or she can outwit the workings of supply and
demand.

Experts will step in where even fools fear to tread.

No speculator can be right all the time. In fact, if a speculator is correct half of the time he is hitting a good average. Even being right three or four times out of ten should yield a person a fortune if he has the sense to cut his losses quickly on ventures where he has been wrong.

I have found it wise, in fact, to periodically turn into cash most of my holdings and virtually retire from the market. No general keeps his troops fighting all the time; nor does he go into battle without some part of his forces held back in reserve.

Early Days

GOT A FEW hundred dollars ahead; I would be cleaned out of everything, my original stake included.

I lost not only my own money but some of Father's as well. On one occasion I felt sure that a fortune could be made in an overhead trolley line that ran between the landing and a hotel at Put-in-Bay on a Lake Erie island. The venture had been brought to my attention by a personally charming promoter named John P. Carrothers, whom Father and I had met on the ship returning from Europe in 1890. I was so carried away that I persuaded Father to invest $8,000, a considerable part of his savings in the scheme. Every dollar was lost.

Although Father never reproached me, the loss weighed on my heart. I imagine I took it much harder than Father, who was more concerned with human values than with money.

Not long after the trolley setback, I remarked to Mother that if I had $500 I could make some money in Tennessee Coal and Iron.

"Why don't you ask Father for it?" she urged.

I protested that after the Put-in-Bay disaster, I could not ask him for another penny.

A few days later Father came to me with a check for $500. Memory plays us subtle tricks and I cannot recall whether or not I accepted the money. That detail is obscured by the larger significance of the incident —the profound lift it was to my self-respect to learn that, after I had cost him so much of his earnings, Father still had faith in me.

Unquestionably, Father was psychologist enough to know something of the struggle going on within me. My mind was in a state of balance where the touch of a hand might swerve me in a direction that could determine the whole course of my career.

In such circumstances, some men grow desperate. I grew cautious. I began a habit I was never to forsake—of analyzing my losses to determine where I had made my mistakes. This was a practice I was to develop ever more systematically as my operations grew in size. After each major undertaking—and particularly when things had turned sour —I would shake loose from Wall Street and go off to some quiet place where I could review what I had done and where I had gone wrong. At such times I never sought to excuse myself but was concerned solely with guarding against a repetition of the same error.

Periodic self-examination of this sort is something all of us need, in both private and governmental affairs. It is always wise for individuals and governments to stop and ask whether we should rush on blindly as in the past. Have new conditions arisen which require a change of direction or pace? Have we lost sight of the essential problem and are we simply wasting our energies on distractions? What have we learned that may help us avoid repeating the same old errors? Also, the more we know of our own failings, the easier it becomes to understand other people and why they act as they do.

In those early days it wasn't too difficult to figure out what I was doing that was wrong. There are two principal mistakes that nearly all amateurs in the stock market make.

The first is to have an inexact knowledge of the securities in which *ne is dealing, to know too little about a company's management, its arnings and prospects for future growth.

The second mistake is to trade beyond one's financial resources, to ry to run up a fortune on a shoestring. That was my main error at the utset. I had virtually no "capital" to start with. When I bought stocks put up so small a margin that a change of a few points would wipe ut my equity. What I was really doing was little more than betting vhether a stock would go up or down. I might be right sometimes, but ny sizable fluctuation would wipe me out.

While I was carrying on these speculations, I had become a bond alesman and customers' man for A. A. Housman & Company. It hap-ened to be a crucial period as far as the country's finances were con-erned. The panic of 1893 closed many mills and mines and put into eceivership a large part of all the railroads in the country. By 1895, nough, one could detect the first promises of better financial weather.

I had never experienced a depression before. But even then I began o grasp dimly that the period of emergence from a depression provides are opportunities for financial profit.

During a depression people come to feel that better times never vill come. They cannot see through their despair to the sunny future nat lies behind the fog. At such times a basic confidence in the coun-ry's future pays off, if one purchases securities and holds them until rosperity returns.

From what I saw, heard, and read, I know that was exactly what the iants of finance and industry were doing. They were quietly acquiring nterests in properties which had defaulted but which would pay out nder competent management once normal economic conditions were estored. I tried to do the same thing with my limited means.

The defaulted securities of railroads interested me particularly— artly I suppose, because the romance of railroading had attracted me rom childhood when the brakemen on the freight trains waved to me s they passed Grandfather's house in Winnsboro. Then, this was also he period during which the nation's railroads, many of which had been wastefully overbuilt, were being consolidated into more efficient properties.

The problem was to determine which securities would survive these reorganizations. Those that did would become immensely valuable. Those that did not would be junked as worthless.

At first I made mistakes in picking the right securities. This spurred me to study the railroads involved more closely. I compiled a list of the railroads being reorganized whose securities seemed to me likely to prove sound investments. To test myself I jotted down in a little black notebook my expectations for these securities.

One entry I made suggested selling New Haven stock and buying Richmond and West Point Terminal, which was later reorganized into what is now the Southern Railway System. Other comments regarding the Atchison, Topeka and Santa Fe and Northern Pacific showed some foresight. Still another successful forecast in my little black book was a prediction that if Union Pacific were bought at the price then prevailing it would pay 100 per cent on the investment when it came out of receivership and was fully developed.

Baruch's 10 Rules

O THER PEOPLE'S MISTAKES, I have noticed, often
make us only more eager to try to do the same
thing. Perhaps it is because in the breast of every
man there burns not only that divine spark of discontent
but the urge to "beat the game" and show himself smarter
than the other fellow. In any case, only after we have
repeated these errors for ourselves does their instructive
effect sink home.

Being so skeptical about the usefulness of advice, I
have been reluctant to lay down any "rules" or guidelines
on how to invest or speculate wisely. Still, there are a
number of things I have learned from my own experience
which might be worth listing for those who are able to
muster the necessary self-discipline:

1. Don't speculate unless you can make it a full-time job.
2. Beware of barbers, beauticians, waiters—of anyone—
   bringing gifts of "inside" information or "tips."
3. Before you buy a security, find out everything you can
   about the company, its management and competitors,
   its earnings and possibilities for growth.

4. Don't try to buy at the bottom and sell at the top. This can't be done—except by liars.

5. Learn how to take your losses quickly and cleanly. Don't expect to be right all the time. If you have made a mistake, cut your losses as quickly as possible.

6. Don't buy too many different securities. Better have only a few investments which can be watched.

7. Make a periodic reappraisal of all your investments to see whether changing developments have altered their prospects.

8. Study your tax position to know when you can sell to greatest advantage.

9. Always keep a good part of your capital in a cash reserve. Never invest all your funds.

10. Don't try to be a jack of all investments. Stick to the field you know best.

These "rules" mainly reflect two lessons that experience has taught me—that getting the facts of a situation before acting is of crucial importance, and that getting these facts is a continuous job which requires eternal vigilance.

GLENN
G. MUNN

Bear Market Technician

Glenn G. Munn was one of Wall Street's "name" writers during the great boom of the Twenties. A widely followed security analyst for Paine, Webber & Co., he wrote several important technical works and edited the Encyclopedia of Banking and Finance. Munn offered some valuable post-mortems on 1929 in his *Meeting the Bear Market,* published by Harper & Bros., 1930.

The Wisdom of
GLENN G. MUNN

"Stocks will find their own level..."

MOTION IS THE first rule of the market. Extremely sensitive to the constant barrage of business news reported by the efficient financial news agencies, and to shifts in floating supply, the stock market is too delicately balanced a mechanism to remain for long on dead center. Almost everything that happens in business has a direct or indirect influence on stock values, and the forces of organized speculation—professional traders, bankers, and investment trusts—are always alert to capitalize changes in the business situation. Beyond the disturbances of purely economic origin are the various sorts of artificial agitation caused by pool manipulation and professional maneuvering. Inertia and stagnation are abhorrent to the speculative fraternity, and conditions within the market itself can be made the basis for price variations when economic motivation is absent.

Stock movements may be classified as (1) primary or cyclical—the major trend movements occupying a period of years and comprehending a complete cycle including a bull and a bear market; (2) secondary—the minor or

ntermediate swings of weeks' or months' duration in which reactions
n a bull market are distinguishable; and (3) tertiary—the superficial
aily ripples ruffling the surface of the secondary waves as the sec-
ndary waves are superimposed on the primary tides. The primary
novements have their source in economic fundamentals, the secondary
novements are chiefly technical but economic in part, while the ter-
iary movements are almost wholly technical. It is with the secondary
nd tertiary movements that the student of technical action is mainly
oncerned.

The Minor Swings

INSIGHT INTO THE nature of speculative movemen
may be had by a rough classification of the intentior
of stock owners. Broadly, two classes are distinguish
able: (1) stocks owned outright, and (2) the floating sup
ply. Stocks held outright are registered in the name of th
owner for the sake of their income and possibilities c
appreciation. There is no immediate intention to sell. The
are placed in safe deposit boxes, and "off the market.
Only potentially do such holdings play a part in the de
termination of prices. As against stock held for permaner
or quasi-permanent investment is the floating supply
This is the balance of the capitalization of a corporatio
without a permanent owner. Such stock is held in margi
accounts, usually against a loan, and is in the name of
broker (street certificates). The floating supply is subjec
to speculative treatment, and the operations of those wh
control the shifting floating supply are the determinant
of short-swing price fluctuations.

Not all the holders of stock have the same intentions, an
a sub-classification of these intentions is here subjoinec

1. Stocks owned outright. (Held for quasi-permanent investment; rarely come on to the market; when sold may be replaced by other issues.)
2. The floating supply. (Held by transient owners.)
    a. Stocks bought with intention of long-pull holding.
    b. Stocks bought with intention of short-swing holding.
    c. Stocks bought by day-to-day (in-and-out) traders.

Speculation for the long pull is founded on the promise of broad primary movements. Speculators so minded base their commitments on fundamentals and analysis. They are not interested in quick trading profits, and from their point of view minor swings are unimportant and day-to-day and week-to-week fluctuations meaningless. But an organized exchange is a daily market and must express itself as a continuous process. No tree grows to heaven in a day, and even in an ebullient market, price advances are never perpendicular. Higher or lower prices may be in the making for the long-pull operator, but the existence of speculators with a trading attitude, willing to accept a few points profits if they accrue within a trading session or overnight, and another group willing to clinch larger profits obtainable within a week or a month, prevent the market from permitting wide gaps in price changes. Continuity is the second law of the market.

Not less than one-fifth and perhaps as much as one-third of the transactions on the stock exchange represent dealings of traders on the floor. Probably no more than 10 per cent of stock exchange members trade exclusively for their own account, but there are many who transact business both for themselves and other members. These are the professional traders who stand ready to take advantage of any item in the news or of changes in technical conditions susceptible of altering a trend. This group is augmented by others, who, though non-members, engage in speculation as a vocation. Since so large a part of total dealings is consummated by those interested in profits from quick turns, daily price variations are seldom extensive in normal markets. A large proportion of professional transactions, indeed, is closed before trading ceases, profit or no profit.

Obviously, the conscious motive of speculators is profits, which may or may not follow. But in their operations, they perform the useful economic function of carrying the floating supply of securities. Profit possibilities are greater in a moving and active market than in an immobile, listless, dormant market. If all speculators were of the long-pull variety, the market would be a dull and colorless exhibition, and for their purposes might be closed until the fruitage they expect has had time to mature. The function of the trading element, then, is to provide a continuous open market, enabling investors (and long-pull holders) to convert their securities into cash at virtually a moment's notice, or to buy in anticipation of an appreciation in values. The trading point of view enlivens the market, affords a basis of operations for investors and long-pull speculative holders, and permits a continuous flow of quotations. It is in this sense, though the ceaseless oscillation of prices composing the tertiary movements seems banal and purposeless, merely reflecting momentary revisions of buyers' and sellers' schedules, that the surface ripples caused by short-run trading are justified.

The attitude of those who are trading-minded is always that if stocks will not move in one direction they must move in the other. If a buying movement on volume, lifting prices a number of points, spends itself, as denoted by diminishing activity on the advance, traders will conclude that the movement will be followed up no further and that prices have temporarily risen as high as they will go. As they take profits and perhaps put out short lines, prices recede. Others may sell, assisting the declining movement. If the selling subsides, and stocks are supported at lower levels, they conclude it is time to cover short lines and to go long of stock. The trading viewpoint is to accept small profits from short swings on the theory that if the capital is turned over frequently, aggregate profits are as great as by assuming a long-pull position.

Trading by the Tape

THE THEORY OF the technicist is that each price change, taken in relation to the volume of trading, has significance—more than that, forecast value. He assumes that there is a meaning behind each purchase and sale, and though the tape does not disclose the source of buying or selling—which admittedly would be helpful —this is of less importance than the fact of buying or selling. Nobody buys or sells without some reason though the reason be impeachable. This is not to say that price and volume changes as unreeled by the tape can always be interpreted in a way to permit profitable trades. There are times when the evidence is negative.

It is also assumed that fundamentals and analysis are incorporated, or are in process of being incorporated, in the price. Any new development in a company's affairs, whether favorable or unfavorable, will begin to register itself in the price of the stock in advance of the announcement of the news. This is because those in a position first to know of impending developments will endeavor to capitalize the information by buying; or, if the news be adverse, by selling. Consequently, when a stock rises on increasing activity, not otherwise explained, there is valid technical reason for following the move. Conversely, if it declines on increasing volume, the technical signal that it should be sold is worth accepting. Taken in totality, these operaions cause similar changes in average prices.

There are many successful traders who derive inspiration almost exclusively from the revelations of the tape, and the daily history of tape action is graphically delineated in chart form. Fundamentals and analysis are important as background and in predicating long-term movements, and need not be ignored, but for secondary and tertiary movements the tape tells the story to one experienced in interpreting its record. The advantage of guidance by technical action is that the trader need have no preconceived idea of the market's future price path. He need have no pattern for the market to follow. Frequently, fundamentals and analysis suggest movement in one direction, but the immediate short-swing movement is in the opposite. The technicist is not disappointed if the market fails to conform to the course predetermined as logical. He takes his signals from the market itself and does not quarrel with it. As a result, he is in step with the market and has no apologies to make if its behavior is counter to preconceptions

---

Sponsorship and Support Levels

FEW LISTED STOCKS are so friendless as to be without a godfather. Virtually every important issue is sponsored by a group (investment bank, investment trust, speculative pool, an individual or individuals, stabilizing account, or the corporation itself), willing to make its market. Sponsorship varies in financial power, but is designed to protect the stock against unjustifiable bear forays, to maintain a price in consonance with its warranted value as a point of honor with the underwriting group's offering price, and for the purpose of accumulation and later distribution. The sponsors are in close touch with the company's progress and presumably in a favored position to know its real worth.

Sponsorship thus gives rise to support points on declines and resistance points on advances. The detection of such points is one of the tasks of the technicist. The sponsors have in mind a minimum price at which their stock should sell under a given set of market conditions, and are prepared to purchase at such a price should it drop thereto.

Referring solely to the movement of the averages, a trading area on a high plateau in a bull market almost invariably is an interlude in what later proves to be a resumption of the rise, else the energy required to hold prices within the area would not have been expended. The technical rule is that the line of least resistance is motion, and stocks having risen to a temporary apex, would be more apt to round off and with little hesitation to start downward. Similarly, a trading area at the bottom of a sharp decline is a breathing space to take account of fundamentals. If the decline has gone too far, recovery, if there is to be one, will lose no time in asserting itself. Consequently, a trading area following a declining movement is usually the precursor of a resumption of the fall. Technically, then, a trading area is a compromise since the rule of motion is violated. It is a concession of technical conditions to fundamentals.

What applies to the averages in regard to trading areas is not applicable to individual stocks. Frequently, what appears to be a trading area at the bottom of a decline in an individual stock is a zone of accumulation with the next important movement upward. Similarly, the semblance of a trading area in an individual stock on a high plateau frequently turns out to be a level of distribution with the next move downward.

A trading area offers one type of market situation in which the trader may have his decision made for him with a minimum of risk. Since a trading area is an interruption of the trend, the market will show, by its own action, what the direction will be when the trading market has terminated. Just as soon as the averages break out of their trading range in one direction or the other, the action can be followed almost blindly. Almost invariably, it is a signal for a continuation of that directional change.

Best Trading Vehicles

TRADERS ABLE TO watch the tape incessantly and who are interested in short-swing (perhaps day-to-day) trading profits, should concentrate their operations in those active leaders which vibrate over the widest diurnal arcs. Activity is essential to insure completion of the round turn. More accurately, they will wish to select the stocks showing the greatest daily movements as a percentage of price (and therefore capital requirement).

Some Technical Principles

I N A BULL market there are important reactions, but unless the bull market has been completed, each succeeding reaction fails to reach the low point of its predecessor. If it does, there is a presumption that the bull market has already passed its crest. Similarly, each intermediate advance in a bull market carries farther than the preceding one. Failure of a secondary advance to pass the high point of its predecessor is a presumption, requiring later confirmation, that a bear market is in the making.

Likewise, in a bear market there are important rallies. Until the major decline has been completed, however, each succeeding rally point falls short of the highest position in the immediately preceding rally. When, finally, a rally lifts itself above the next preceding one, there is presumptive, but not conclusive, evidence that the major trend has been reversed.

One month of record-breaking movement in the averages is never followed by another in succession, although the trend may be in the same direction. This holds true in both rising and falling markets. The rapid rise in June, 1929, was followed by a trading market in July. The record-breaking rise in August, 1929, was followed by a decline in September. The unprecedented decline of October, 1929, was followed by an additional, but far less drastic, decline in November.

An almost infallible clue to the end of an intermediate bull swing is the sudden collapse of some popular but overexploited issue. Since 1926, practically every intermediate reaction was heralded by such an incident. In each instance, a sharp decline in Devoe & Reynolds, Manhattan Electric Supply, Bancitaly, Canadian Marconi and Advance Rumely were harbingers of important reactions in this period. Another sign is an unexplained downturn in the entire list.

The culmination of an intermediate or major reaction never appears on heavy trading volume. There may be temporary pauses and recoveries, but so long as activity persists, it is practically certain that bottom has not yet been reached. The conclusion is detected by an evaporation of liquidation in coincidence with a material contraction in sales volume. When diminished turnover is accompanied by narrow price movements, the basal point of the break has been approached and a foundation established for a fresh advance. There is no rule by which to determine the interval that must elapse to start the recovery. It is seldom delayed for long. It will be first suggested by the appearance of strength in a number of leaders or a certain group of stocks that happens to be relatively favorably situated.

In a declining market, when 80 per cent or more of the stocks showing changes for the day are minus three days successively (ignoring issues showing no change for the day), a rally in the nature of a spontaneous automatic rebound must be expected. The normal rally from the low point in a declining phase is from one-third to one-half of the distance lost from the preceding high point. When, in a declining market, stocks are purchased in the climax period, the safe procedure is to dispose of them on the ensuing rally.

A zigzag movement in which stocks travel up and down in a single session without dislocating the general range, is neutral and inconclusive evidence of the next directional change. When price movements are inconclusive, the trader, in an endeavor to detect a favorable buying point, may await one of three developments: (1) A sharp decline of climactic proportions on increasing activity (which should spend itself on the third day); (2) a drying up of the reactionary tendency, as evidenced by dullness and narrow price fluctuations; or (3) the rising of prices to a point just above the last preceding resistance levels through which they were unable to penetrate.

Neither the market as a whole nor an individual stock normally rises perpendicularly even in a bull market; considered from either point of view, the market rarely proceeds in one direction more than five consecutive days without encountering some degree of reaction, however trifling.

Technically, the market tries for continuity. Gaps (when the price range of one day is wholly detached from the preceding day) are against the law of continuity. Unless there is overnight news in explanation, there is always a strong tendency for the gap to be closed, irrespective of the direction. The reason is that an unexplained decline will attract buying by the trading element; a sudden rise induces selling.

Accumulation, especially careful accumulation, is more likely to take place in markets of relatively small volume; distribution on heavy volume.

It is a Wall Street maxim that a short position should be covered in case unfavorable news, other than that expected, permits of this procedure.

Part IV

Sages of the Thirties...

Despite the slow recovery, trading continued on Wall Street. Everything was on a much reduced scale, of course, as compared with the great speculative binge of the Twenties. But even in the Thirties traders tried to take profits out of the market.

To do so, there had to be a refinement of the rules, conceived in the orientation of a depressed market place.

GEORGE SEAMAN . . Compiler of Trading Rules.

RICHARD W. SCHABACKER . . Pioneer of Sophisticated Technical Research.

HAROLD M. GARTLEY . . Master Market Technician.

GEORGE
SEAMAN

Compiler of Trading Rules

One notable attempt at developing new rules, firmly grounded in the speculative techniques of the Twenties and the more somber approaches of the Thirties, was found in *The Seven Pillars of Stock Market Success*, published by Seamans-Blake, Chicago, 1933. The original edition was anonymous, but subsequent editions carried the name of George Seaman. The book included his celebrated "100 Rules" which became standard market philosophy in the 1930's. Many of the "rules" are often referred to in today's market literature, although Seaman is seldom acknowledged as their original compiler.

The Wisdom of
GEORGE SEAMAN

Unchanging Laws of the Market

RULE 1.   In the beginning, trade only in an imaginary way instead of with money. After you have read this book and feel that you have learned a great deal, prove it to yourself by buying and selling stocks **but without money.** Enter every purchase order in a ledger, as though you had given the order to your broker, tabulating a half point for commission and taxes. Execute your buying and selling as though you were playing for real money. Do not fool yourself and do not try to fool your ledger. After a few months of this kind of playing, make out your balance sheet. Figure how many times you were right and how many times you were wrong. If the **times right** exceed the **times wrong** (not how much money you won or lost), go ahead and play for money. Do not play with very much at the beginning. Ten shares is quite sufficient; if you come out ahead this will give you confidence in yourself. Then you can increase your trading to 100 share lots or to any amount within your means.

(Probably each of my readers will have the tendency to think, as I did, that he is different; that he does not have to go through a period of training and apprenticeship. Very quickly I found I was mistaken.)

Rule 2.   When you begin to trade make up your mind that a good part of your capital will be lost before you make a success. (That is Wall Street's usual charge for "breaking" you in.) It is only by practice and study that you will learn how to play the market. Naturally, you will make plenty of mistakes. Therefore, if you have, let us say, $10,000.00 at the time of your initiation, figure that you will lose part of it before you make much headway. That is why I strongly urge that in the beginning you trade only in ten share lots rather than in one hundred share lots. Learn the market at the lowest possible tuition fee. You have time to play in 100 or 1,000 share lots after you have learned how to trade. Should you start with 100 or 1,000 share lots, you will not have enough money left after you have learned. **So start low and grow as you go along.**

(In the beginning of your trading career read Rule No. 2. daily. It will give you much comfort and peace and money to play with, when you graduate.)

Rule 3.   Do not deal in inactive stocks. Play with live ones. (When you sleep with a dog you awake with fleas.)

Rule 4.   Do not hold on to a stock if you see it dropping; it may drop more. You may be able to buy more stock at the bottom for the same money.

(There is no valid reason to hold a stock just because you bought it.)

Rule 5.   Do not be overly enthusiastic and permit your prospective profits to run away with you, hoping that stocks will go up still further. **Hope** is your worst enemy in the market. The public usually observes its stocks dropping, hoping against hope that they will advance or make a comeback. But this rarely happens soon enough.

Rule 6.   Do not play in low-priced stocks. Keep away from stocks that have not reached a $20 high for a year or so. The best stocks to play with are those from $30 to $130. On higher priced stocks like U. S. Steel or Chrysler, the chances of making money quickly are more certain.

(Always pick a winner.)

Rule 7.   Never cover a margin call. Why put good money after bad? You are not saving anything by putting up more money on your margin. In the final analysis the value of your stock at your broker's is what it can be sold for at market, at the **present moment.** Use your reasoning powers and you will agree you are not helping your situation any, because, if your stock dropped 40% or 50% it may drop still more. You must admit that if you are called upon to put up more margin money it means either that you have bought poor stock, or that you bought at a wrong time. In either case the additional mistake of "hanging on" until the margin bugle blows is fatal, and you should liquidate your purchase. Start trading anew by buying the **right stock** at the **right time.**

(If someone owed you money and you could not collect, would you loan him more money?)

Rule 8.   If you have been "unlucky" in the market, do not try to play with the thought in the back of your mind of making up your losses—forget about them. As a matter of fact, if you have been unlucky for any length of time, the best thing to do is to stop and get away from the market for awhile. Think over what you have done which caused these losses. Perform a post-mortem. When your mind feels rested, and you have forgotten about your losses, you can begin again, but **not with the view of making up your losses.** Play with the view of making money.

Rule 9.   If you have a loss on the market on, let us say, 100 shares, do not play 200 or 300 shares in order to make up your previous losses in a hurry. You may have another and bigger loss than before. Just keep on playing 100 shares as you played on the losing side. Never try to take revenge on the market. You will never do well in that frame of mind. Let me repeat: play the market because you want to make money and because it is ripe for a play, not because you want to make up your losses. Otherwise it will lead you into taking undue chances and usually you will be the loser. The market must be played according to the laws you have learned, and without sentiment.

Rule 10. Do not jump around from one stock to another thinking the grass is greener in one place than in another. It is not. It is better to play a few stocks and learn their habits well.

Rule 11. Remember that it takes years to learn how to trade properly and to learn how to interpret the tape. Do not expect to make millions in one week or one year. It takes practice to become perfect.

Rule 12. Never take the advice or act exclusively on the opinion of any advisory service. I subscribe to about ten and they hardly ever agree. Learn to give yourself your own advice, based on knowledge.

(Why should they know more than you?)

Rule 13. The best broker is the one who will not give you advice. A good broker should take instructions and let you use your own judgment.

Rule 14. When you see the market advance, do not rush to buy. This may be the end of the advance and you will be buying at top prices. Wait until a reaction sets in—then buy.

(Those who buy on reactions sell out on advances. Those who buy on advances sell out on reactions.)

Rule 15. Never ask anybody's advice or think that the next fellow knows more than you. If you follow his advice you may as well give him your money to trade with, which of course, you would not do. Then why ask his advice? Learn to do your own thinking and develop sufficient confidence in yourself to enable you to rely on your own judgment. Solve your problems. In time you will be solving other people's problems.

Rule 16.   Do not let anyone influence you when you have made a decision to buy or get out. Act according to your convictions.

Rule 17.   Do not trade on "tips" given by friends, by your broker, or on rumors flying around broker's offices.

Rule 18.   Change your position quickly if you see that you are wrong. It is better to take a small loss rather than wait until your losses increase. When you buy for a ten point rise, and the stock does not do well, close out at a small profit or loss. Do not stick to a stock just because you bought it. You should be proud of your ability at catching your mistakes in time. A few hours may make all the difference.

(Remember October, 1937.)

Rule 19.   Do not buy a stock because the price is low. A stock is only cheap if you can sell it at a higher price. The difference between cheap and expensive is not the **price** but the **time** element. There are times when a stock at $75 is cheap and other times when the same stock at $25 is expensive. To be successful it is not as important to know what to buy as **when** to buy. The price you pay at the "right" time is no criterion so long as you can sell at a higher price.

Rule 20.   Do not gamble. Speculation is **not** gambling. A gambler is one who does not know what to do and therefore takes chances. A speculator is one who knows what it is all about, although often he, too, gets "stung." A gambler has little knowledge and bases everything on luck. A speculator who trades according to the laws of the market wins three times out of five and needs no luck.

(If you must satisfy your gambling instincts play solitaire, it is much cheaper.)

Rule 21.   Do not over-trade. Always play with sufficient margin so that your broker cannot sell you out. Do not take advantage of any more than half the legal margin allowance, and during uncertain times trade with no margin at all. Pay for your stocks outright. And buy only with part of your capital.

Rule 22. Do not play with somebody else's money, whether it is your broker's or your friend's, or with money which you can ill-afford to lose.

Rule 23. If you are attempting to make money in a hurry you will not succeed. There is money in Wall Street for you and if you do not get it today you will get it a week or a month hence. You have a better chance to get it, however, if you wait. Play when the T!ME is ripe.

(A hundred yard dash may get you out of breath.)

Rule 24. Do not be discouraged if you make mistakes. The best traders do. Learn from those mistakes and try not to repeat them. Attempt to find out the underlying cause. When you have thoroughly reasoned out what you did or failed to do, resolve not to make the same error again. Do not place faith in luck, because if you think it is luck that makes the market go up or down you will never be a successful trader. The market has its reasons for going up and down. It is up to you to find them out.

(We all make mistakes but only a fool or a weakling repeats them.)

Rule 25. Be skeptical about any trade that appears to be a dead-sure winner. When you feel one hundred percent certain that you will come out well, that is just the time to look around with a critical eye. Never be **dead sure**. The market may have a lot of surprises in store for you.

(More people get stung by "sure things" than by bees.)

Rule 26. Do not attempt to "guess" the market. Play only because you have come to definite conclusions by analysis of the situation. Do not arrive at these conclusions without first measuring every angle by fundamental economic conditions, the trend, Dow Theory, and the signals from your charts. When these are in your favor, weigh the news items in your paper to determine if this is the psychological moment to make your purchase.

Rule 27. Bear in mind always that the market is in the strongest technical position when it is "weak" with prices down and news gloomy. Moreover, it is in an extremely weak position when it appears to be strongest, as when prices are up, business booming and newspapers full of prosperity psychology. Following the theory of cycles, it works out thus: those who are strong have **potential** weakness which must assert itself sooner or later, those that are momentarily weak, possess potential strength.

(Remember what Jesus said about the strength of those who are weak and about the weakness of those who are strong.)

Rule 28.   If you want to come out ahead, do not repeat your mistakes. In that way eventually you will succeed. Remember, also, that the market always gives you a thousand and one opportunities to make new errors. So be on guard!

Rule 29.   It is advisable to play with not more than ten stocks. Study these stocks painstakingly, their actions for years back, their resistance points, and their behavior, so that you may know exactly what they are capable of doing. Ordinarily, what holds good for the entire market, will hold true for your particular stock. Whatever you trade in should be among the ten best sellers on the Exchange. It is advisable to deal only in issues which have a wide market and move rapidly. Select any of the fast leaders for a particular week or month. It is true that at times some stocks have advantages over others, but they are all subject to the same law of supply and demand. There is no reason to play with 100 different stocks, when you can play with a few which you know intimately.

(Remember that the devil you know is better than the devil you do not know.)

Rule 30.   Do not average your stock if it goes against you. Do not buy more of the same stock at a lower price if it has already dropped. Close it out instead.

(A dried up cow goes to the butcher.)

Rule 31.   Place your "stops" so that they will be ⅛ below even figures on a "long" buy, and ⅛ above even figures on a "short." Place your stops below resistance points on a "long" buy and above resistance points on a "short" sale.

(Even then they may "gun" for you.)

Rule 32.   Your success in speculative operations on the Exchange is based on the following: First, on your ability to determine economic and political conditions, not as they are today, but as they will be three to six months hence. Second, your ability to determine what certain pools and manipulators in Wall Street are doing or intend to do with the stocks they have on hand or with the stocks in the hands of the public. If, after a thorough study of the situation, you decide that Wall Street is interested in buying, then do the same. If, on the contrary, they are disposing of their holdings, sell yours and go short, especially if you detect the move at the top.

Rule 33.   To purchase or sell short any stock, begin with the assumption that your profits will be four to five times your risk. If you expect only a two point rise, do not buy. Wait until your analysis shows clearly a possible advance of 8 to 10 points. Then risk two points on a five-to-one shot. This is much better than a one-to-one chance.

(A one-to-one shot is gambling. A five-to-one shot is speculating.)

Rule 34.   Money can best be made when buying on the down of a move and then selling close to the top. If you have predetermined by analysis the resistance points on the particular stock you are dealing in, the possibility of error is limited.

Rule 35.   Always purchase stocks in the strongest groups. There are times when some groups are stronger than others, when railroads are weak and industrials strong, and when coppers are strong and foods weak. Therefore, always buy in the strongest group. Determine this from the action of the market. The stronger groups will advance further or offer more resistance to decline than the weaker groups. In each group there are always one or two stocks that do better on an average than the group as a whole. That is the stock you should buy for an upward pull. On the other hand, if you wish to play the market short, choose a weak group, one that has not been doing well. Select the weakest stock in that group (the one most sensitive to decline) for a short play.

Rule 36.   Trade evenly. Do not buy 100 shares today and 1000 shares tomorrow. If you trade in 100 share lots do not buy more than 100 shares unless you decide to advance in general your scope of trading. Your percentage of winners or losers will not work out if you vary the amounts from time to time. For example: if out of ten trades in 100 share lots you have had seven winners, and then you play with a 1000 share lot and sustain one loss, this will wipe out all your seven winnings. However, if you stick to 100 share lots and you have a loss, you will have six winners and only one loser.

(Be in balance.)

Rule 37.   The most important thing in the market is the "trend." Do not attempt to trade until you are able to deduce this from a thorough analysis. **Always trade with the trend and not against the trend.** If the trend is doubtful, stay out of the market entirely until the trend is visible, even if it takes weeks or months. You will be well compensated by not trading in a market of which you are in doubt. Money is not made by being in all the time. (In fact that is a good way of losing it.) One or two good trades a month will net you more than trading day in and day out on guess-work.

Rule 38.   Learn to be patient. Guard against hurry-skurry. If you have calculated that your stock will move up a certain number of points and you think that you are correct in your theory, have the patience to wait. Your opportunity may arrive just five minutes after you have sold out your stocks at a lower figure.

(The world might very well have been destroyed in the days of Lot if the good Lord were without patience. So says the Book of Books.)

Rule 39.   Do not permit your opinions about political matters to influence your market judgment. You may have a soft spot for the underdog and sympathize with the New Deal. But during market hours consider President Roosevelt's speeches and actions objectively so that you may gauge every possibility and reaction. Learn to exercise professional judgment and do not allow your political opinions to interfere with your stock market trading.

("When in Rome do as the Romans do.")

Rule 40.   When the tape has been going in a certain direction, either up, or down, and it comes to a stop for a few seconds, that usually signifies that a new chapter is starting. Sometimes it may be a stronger continuation in the same direction. More often, however, it indicates that the market will very soon turn in the opposite direction.

Rule 41.   Remember that the reason stocks go up and down is basically because of **supply and demand.** If there are more buyers than sellers, stocks will go up, even though they were on the downward trend. Some people may wish to sell, but if the people who buy are more numerous and have more money, stocks naturally will go up. When stocks do go up, it is because people want to pay the price. In other words, the demand is greater than the supply. When a point is reached where there are no more buyers at the prices asked, then the demand has diminished. From that point on a decline will take place. With this in mind, act accordingly. When you notice that the supply is greater than the demand and stocks begin to drop, **sell.** You cannot be certain how far they will go down, because you cannot measure how great the supply is and whether the demand will be strong enough to stop this supply. Your most logical move under such circumstances, is to sell. This holds good particularly in an uncertain or down trend market.

(There are exceptions to every rule. The prudent trader will break thi sound rule under justifiable circumstances.)

Rule 42.   Do not ride up and down with a stock. Although you ma have bought with the idea that it will go up ten points, that is no reasor why you should wait for the ten points and not take profits beforehand if they are available. If you bought at 100 with the object of selling a 110 and have followed to 105 (half way) a corrective reaction may b in order. That stock may want to test the 102-103 level. Is there an reason why you should let it ride down on you? The commissions are approximately, only a half point. The wisest thing to do is to sell at 105 buy back at 102-103-104 or even 105. Do not stay with it while it i reacting as it may go below 100. This gives you the followin advantages:

1) A chance to buy for less, thereby making additional profits.
2) Taking no chances while it is slipping on the way down.
3) If the stock should react to 103-104 and then shoot up to 106, it i a safe buy at 106. It has already gone through the reaction anc you know that it will go up.

(Remember, you do not marry a stock when you buy, nor do you pay alimony on parting.)

Rule 43.   Watch commodity prices every day, especially wheat anc cotton. Take particular note of bank issues. If they go down, most likely all other stocks will go down. The same is true of commodities. A drop in commodity prices usually foretells a drop in stock prices. Another item to watch is foreign selling. During 1937 there was considerable foreign buying and selling. The buying was during the beginning of the year and the selling during the latter part. Many breaks in the market were due to foreign selling.

Rule 44.   It is advisable to place a **time** ultimatum on stocks you buy. If a stock does not come up to your expectations within a certain time, sell, even at a loss. You cannot afford to have your money tied up or too long a period. Meanwhile you may be losing the profits which you could have made if you had invested in other stocks, which are in their technical up move.

Rule 45.   Do not take money out of your business to trade on the market unless your business can unquestionably do without it. Do not play the market with money which will cause you too great anxiety. You will never succeed when you are in that state of mind.

Rule 46.   Do not try to squeeze out the last quarter or half point. If you have made a profit and feel it will not go much higher, it is best to sell and pocket your profits. Potential profits do not mean anything; it is only the money you have after you have sold your stocks that count.

Rule 47.   When you decide to take profits by selling, do it on the up-movement, while the stock is climbing. Do not wait until the movement exhausts itself, as you will then have to sell for one-half or one point less.

(Strike while the iron is hot.)

Rule 48.   When the market is in an **up-trend** and you wish to take advantage of a little shake-out on a reaction, play short, but only with $1/3$ of the amount on the long side. If you purchased 300 shares on the upside, for instance, and decide to sell, dispose of 400 shares. This will mean that you are 100 shares short. When the market has gone down a few points, and you think it will make a turn for a rise, buy 400 shares. This will place you in the position of having covered your 100 short and you will be 300 long. The reverse is true of a down-trend market.

Rule 49.   When buying on a reaction, if the tape moves fast it is best to buy at a stipulated price under the market instead of "at market." Frequently it is advisable to buy or sell "at market," as otherwise you may not get your price and an opportunity may be lost.

Rule 50.   **It is very important** that you know before buying or selling where the next resistance point will be on the averages (Dow-Jones or others) and on the stock you are trading in. For instance: if your records show that there was a good deal of resistance at 102 on Steel you should not buy Steel at 101, as it will certainly sell off at 102 or 103 You should buy at 95; by following it up to 103 and then selling, you can make a profit. The same is true for the Dow-Jones averages. If on previous occasions there was a resistance at 190 on the Dow-Jones averages, sell at 188-189. Buy at 185.

Rule 51.   The chances for covering when playing short are better on a stock with a large number of shares outstanding, such as U. S. Steel Others with a small issue of shares may jump a point or two between sales. So do not short stocks with limited shares.

Rule 52.   The secret of successful stock market operation is to limit your losses as much as possible. Your profits will pyramid.

Rule 53.   When you see a sharp move on the market it is either short covering on the up-side, or purely technical reaction on the down side. Do not let these sudden moves tempt you to go in.

Rule 54.   Watch the higher-priced leaders carefully. A lot of maneuvering on smaller issues frequently transpires with a view to advantageous sales, by having the leaders make a smoke-screen demonstration of strength.

Rule 55.   A good time to sell stocks is on a late tape on an up-market. A good time to cover is on a late tape in a down-market.

Rule 56.   It is not good policy to be long and short at the same time. There were occasions during the month of October 1937, when it was logical to assume that industrials might rise and rails decline. However, it is dangerous to play the market that way. It is best to follow the trend. Remember that rails and industrials must eventually confirm one another.

Rule 57.   In the market be neither a bear nor a bull—have no prejudices. Do not love one side more than the other. Play the up-side or the down-side. If the market is on a down-trend play the short side; if the market is on an up-trend, play the long side. Never try to buck the trend of the market because you feel bullish or bearish. Forget your feelings. Go the way the market goes. Float with it, and the tide will carry you in to shore. The public finds it more pleasant to play the upside. They usually buy stocks in order to advance. The fact of the matter is that the short side often is more profitable, and quicker, because when stocks drop they drop rapidly. Be as much at ease trading on the short side as on the long.

Rule 58. Do not purchase stocks by statistics. The statistical tabulation of a stock does not make it a good or bad buy. It is **now** that counts and not what **has been.** Statistics show only what **has been.** Knowledge of economics is necessary in order to know what is going on **now.** Base your opinion on that and not on statistics. Economics is alive. Statistics are past history—dead documents covered with dust. Quite frequently a stock is in a statistically favorable position, and still it sells lower than the stock which is statistically unsound. **Price is based on supply and demand** not on statistics.

(In a controversy both sides make use of statistics to prove themselves right.)

Rule 59. Remember that the market may do the unexpected. Therefore, always expect the unexpected—not what you would like it to do. Do not trade by wish-fulfillment.

Rule 60. Do not buy or sell the first hour of the market, nor at opening prices, unless extraordinary circumstances prevail. After an hour there has usually been a buying and selling period. From these two periods you can decide more readily whether your contemplated action is timely.

The Seven Pillars

There are **SEVEN PILLARS OF STOCK MARKET PRACTICE** necessary for success. The sixty Rules formulated in the foregoing chapters are based on seven cardinal principles which are the main arteries to successful market trading, e.g.,

1. Determine whether the market is in a "bear" or "bull" trend. Then determine further whether it is a major, intermediate, or minor trend.
    TRADE WITH THE TREND!

2. Determine which groups of stocks are the strongest.
    TRADE IN STRONG GROUPS FOR ADVANCE!
    TRADE IN WEAK GROUPS FOR DECLINE!

3. Select the strongest stocks in these particular groups.
    TRADE IN STRONG STOCKS FOR ADVANCE!
    TRADE IN WEAK STOCKS FOR DECLINE!

4. **BUY ONLY ON REACTIONS**—not on advances!
    SELL AND SHORT ONLY ON ADVANCES—not on declines!

5. Place a mental or (if you do not watch the tape) actual stop-loss order of two or three points on your trades.
    BE AT ALL TIMES PROTECTED AGAINST POSSIBLE LOSSES!
    CLOSE OUT WHEN TRADE GOES AGAINST YOU.

6. Protect your profits by stop-loss orders. Let your profits grow when you see your stocks advancing.
    HOLD OUT FOR LARGER PROFITS!

7. Do not hesitate to take your profits; you may be able to re-buy the same stock at lower prices.
    SELL WHEN YOU THINK THE MARKET IS DUE
    FOR A REACTION!
    SELL AT THE TOP   * * * NOT AT THE BOTTOM
    BUY AT THE BOTTOM   NOT AT THE TOP
    To capitalize on these rules
    reread
    THE SEVEN PILLARS OF STOCK MARKET SUCCESS

RICHARD W. SCHABACKER

Pioneer of Sophisticated Technical Research

R. W. Schabacker may be unknown to many present day investors; yet, his understanding of the market was awesomely profound and his writings on the market perhaps more prolific and technical than any other of his day. Probably the reason Schabacker is not better known is that he wrote during the early Thirties, when public interest in the stock market was at its lowest ebb in all stock exchange history, and when even Charles Dow himself might not have made much of an impression.

Schabacker, born in 1899 in Erie, Pennsylvania attended Princeton University and was graduated cum laude with a B.A. in 1921.

His early positions were with the Federal Reserve Bank of New York, the Standard Statistics Company (now Standard & Poor's) and the Cleveland *Plain Dealer*. In 1925, Schabacker joined *Forbes Magazine*, became the youngest Financial Editor in its history, and remained there for ten years, until his untimely death in 1935 at the age of 36.

During his short but brilliant career, Schabacker authored three books. His *Stock Market Theory and Practice* (published by B. C. Forbes Publishing Co. in 1930), a massive work of 650 pages, was hailed in the New York *Post* as an "encyclopedia on the stock market, indispensable to any financial library." *Technical Analysis and Market*

Profits was published as a mail order course of lessons in 1932. In 1934 came his *Stock Market Profits,* also published by Forbes.

This body of work by Schabacker is among the most influential ever written on the technical side of the market. Recognized as one of the "greats" by market students, his theories were the basic source material used by Edwards and Magee in their standard technical market works. Schabacker pioneered in the discovery of the chart patterns so widely used by technicians today—"head and shoulders," "double top," "Trendlines," etc.

Schabacker also rated as one of the supreme market forecasters of his time; his published forecasts in September 1929, at the peak of the long Bull market, warned of an "impending major reaction" and advised liquidation of stocks.

The Wisdom of
RICHARD W. SCHABACKER

Characteristics of the End of a Bull Market

(From Stock Market Theory and Practice, B. C. Forbes Pub. Co., 1930)

AFTER FUNDAMENTALS HAVE turned unfavorable the technical strength of the market often carries it on up for a much longer period of time and for much wider gains, and only the technical considerations give much clue, in the final analysis, to the time when the market will actually turn. Excitement is one of the strongest evidences of weakening technical position in such a period. Volume of sales mounts to huge figures, tremendous advances take place in individual and speculative favorites, perhaps sudden collapses of other stocks occur at the same time, interest rates are high and call money soars nervously to abnormal heights. Traders begin to get nervous themselves and warnings appear in the newspapers.

But public enthusiasm and the gambling spirit are aroused. People no longer trade for investment, for yield, for fundamental values, or even for small profits. They buy stocks because they think they are going up rapidly and without regard to asset worth or dividends, earnings, true prospects or dividend yield. Tips and rumors run wild.

This stock is going to 500. That one is going up 50 points next week, etc. The stock market "makes the front page" of the newspapers. Everyone is talking stocks. Everyone is in the market or wants to be. And all such circumstances are the most dangerous of symptoms and the very best reasons why the average trader or investor should be selling his stocks rather than buying more. Such circumstances make up the usual picture of the closing days of a long Bull market.

Beginnings of a Bear Market

WHEN THE DISTRIBUTION period is over at the close of any bull market and the major movement has turned downward into the marking down stage or a major bear movement, the tendencies which we have noted in our description of the end of a bull market grow gradually but steadily less potent and less noticeable, finally giving way to just the opposite tendencies, which again go too far the other way at the end of a long bear market.

In the early stages of the bear market, for instance, interest rates are generally still very high, quite often higher than before the bear movement started; business is still satisfactory, or even apparently booming, in individual lines; tips and rumors of a favorable nature are still going around, with frequent sharp recoveries, all perhaps designed to keep the public from becoming discouraged too soon and selling out at comparatively high prices.

As the major bear movement continues interest rates decline, business is poor, commodity prices are often exceptionally low, public confidence is gradually being undermined, earning statements are declining, public interest in the market has dropped away rapidly (at least so far as constructive purchases are concerned), brokers' loans are being reduced, favorable tips and rumors gradually diminish and give way to growing unfavorable ones. Gradually the basic fundamentals are being restored to a more favorable basis, but the public, as usual, sees only the terrific declines, the staggering losses, the growing blackness of the future outlook, just as it saw only the bright side of things while the fundamentals were weakening.

Characteristics of the End of a Bear Market

FINALLY, WHAT IS the picture at the end of the long bear market? Interest rates have been easy for some time, perhaps a year or more, commodity prices are low, wages are far below their previous highs, public buying of all kinds is at low ebb, corporations are trying to liquidate costly inventories and loans, their earnings are poor, even the strongest of companies perhaps showing huge deficits. Dividends are being reduced, failures are on the upgrade, stock prices have dropped for so long that there seems no end.

Now the market "makes the front page" because of its declines instead of its advances. Now the tips and rumors are all on the unfavorable side. This stock is going to have to cut its dividend or pass it. That stock is still too high and is going to drop another 25 points in the next few weeks. This company is on the verge of a receivership and is going bankrupt; that brokerage house is on the ragged edge and likely to join the numerous previous brokerage failures which have already occurred. Even the Twelfth Village Bank is whispered to be in sore difficulties and likely to go under. The country has suffered a death blow. Prosperity may come back some day but it will be a long, hard pull and there is no telling how much further down stocks are going before the turn comes.

What is the result? Just what the insiders are working for. Public confidence is demoralized. The average investor is tied up with his heavy load of stocks accumulated in those rosy days, now seemingly gone forever, when stocks were selling even further above their true asset worth than they are now selling below that worth. The professional speculator, the trader, the wise long swing investor, all have sold their stocks, though perhaps at huge losses, long ago.

Now comes the danger for the long pull investor. Yes, he bought with the idea that nothing could induce him to sell. He was going to hold for long-pull appreciation and pay no attention to intermediate reactions. But now—why, the country is going to the dogs, the stocks that looked so good a year or two ago now look weak enough for receivership. Selling would mean a tremendous loss, but maybe if he sells now he can recoup some of his losses by buying his stocks back later at still lower prices, after things have cleared up a bit.

This is the tragedy of the long-pull investor. It is no exaggeration to say that the greatest amount of public selling is done in such a situation, just when stocks ought to be bought instead of sold, just when inside accumulation is about completed, when the long bear market is about ready to reverse itself into a bull movement. The public usually sells at this seemingly darkest moment, when stocks should be bought for the long-swing, just as it usually buys at the seemingly brightest moment, when long-swing stock holdings ought to be sold.

These pictures may give the reader a rather skeptical outlook on all stock market operations. What they are designed to do is to give him a skeptical attitude toward stock market gossip, publicity and psychology. And if the reader learns from such pictures to discount all he hears as gossip and to base his market activities upon study, experience and fundamental reasoning, then this work will not have been in vain.

Price–Discounting News

BY THE TIME news regarding a stock is made public such news has generally been discounted in the market and the "cream is off."

Take the example of Kennecott Copper, which raised its dividend from $4 to $5 per share in June, 1929. At the beginning of the year the new stock was selling below 80. Copper prices had been advancing and continued to advance. The presumption was that Kennecott's profits were rising since business was also improving with the advance in prices. The fundamentals, therefore, indicated that when such profits became publicly known the popularity of Kennecott stock would be increased and its market valuation would advance. The dividend increase was generally considered a bullish factor.

We know however, that the real bullish factor was the increase in profits. But most of the advance in the stock from 78 to 105 came before the increase in earnings was made public. To this extent the market had already discounted the increase. The time to buy was at the beginning of the year before such increase had been publicly realized. When the dividend was actually raised in June the stock was already back in the 80's.

The next problem was not how much earnings had increased in 1928, but how much more they would increase in 1929. The future movement of the stock depended no longer on past results but on future earnings. And such future earnings depended largely upon the price of copper and the amount of business done. In April the price of copper declined sharply. To a large degree the price of Kennecott declined along with the price of copper.

But the greatest profits on the short side of the stock went to the insiders or to the students of the situation who could forecast the price of copper and Kennecott's future earnings in advance of the time such factors would influence public selling. By the time the price of copper had declined and the dividend was raised Kennecott had dropped back from a high of around 105 to a price of below 80. Once more profits and not dividends were the chief market factor. And the trader whose campaign in Kennecott was successful was the trader who could look far enough ahead to see what the public attitude would be toward Kennecott a couple of weeks or a couple of months from the time he took his own action in discounting that future popularity.

Since the nature of the general and individual market is to discount the future, **its nature is also to stop discounting when the news is out —when the future has become the present.** There are several theoretical angles of this occurrence, which is a fairly general rule. The truly big traders, the important operators, the professional students, all are the big factors in price fluctuations, prior to public participation. This is the "they" crowd in stock market parlance. "They" are the ones who discount the future. "They" influence the market action of the stock to a considerable degree.

If "they" have been buying the stock and advancing the price to discount announcement of favorable earnings, their natural gesture is to get out of the stock and take their profits when such news becomes public. They held the stock in anticipation of public demand. When the good news is out the public should theoretically, and practically does, step in and buy the stock—generally too late. The best time to sell the stock, therefore, is at the time when this public demand should appear. These important interests, who either have intimate foreknowledge, or accurate foresight, and whom we shall call "insiders," have no further reason for holding their previously purchased stock. "They" have a profit in it and the logical time to sell is while the public is still buying on the good news. The result is the somewhat technical tendency for a stock to react, instead of advance, when a piece of good news comes out.

"Be an Insider"

THE STOCK MARKET is made up, generally, of two large groups, the insiders and the public. The insiders are by far the more intelligent, the more experienced, the more professional, with reference to market affairs. They make more or less a business of making money in the stock market.

It is not necessarily the case that one of these groups must lose in order that the other may win. But in perhaps the majority of cases that is what happens. In any case, the two groups are more likely to be working in diametrically opposite directions. When the insiders are buying stocks they are buying them from the public because they expect to sell them back to the public at higher prices. If the insiders are right the public loses again. Of course, the insiders are by no means always right. They often take losses, and when they do they are generally tremendously larger than the small losses that the public is likely to take.

It cannot, of course, be proven that the insiders are right much more often than the public, but it stands to reason that they are in a better position to do the right thing than is the public. And, likewise, the insiders would hardly continue to give so great a portion of their time to their professional activities if they were not able to make average or fairly consistent profits at the end of successive years.

The author does not mean to give the impression that the public is constantly on the wrong side of the market. It cannot be, for it makes the market in a large degree. The insiders cannot pursue any course very long if they do not have public backing. In the majority of cases both groups, the insiders and the public, are making money. But where there is any sharp differentiation it is more likely that the insiders are on the right side.

And, furthermore, it is important to be one of the insiders, or at least to know what they are doing, because it is that group which generally originates major moves. With better background, greater experience, more practice, and often almost unlimited resources to carry through a campaign, the insider group is very likely to begin discounting the future before the public. Once more, the author does not mean that one must be on the inside to make stock market profits. Far from it, the greatest estates have been built up merely by farsighted investment buying of stocks. But for successful market trading it is an advantage to have the facilities which the insiders have.

The beginner may feel that because he is not the officer of a large corporation, not in the customer's room of a large New York stock exchange commission house, his chances for trading profit are dubious. That is not true. In general, it is true that the corporation officer and the customers' man have opportunities for getting information before it is generally known to the public and they thus have some advantages over the ordinary trader. But such "tips" often go astray, and it is by no means sufficient to rely solely upon such inside information in trading.

As a matter of fact, the author uses the term "insider" to denote not merely this small group which has access to private information, but also to denote the trader who has made a study of trading methods, who is more grounded in fundamental theory and technical practice than the "man in the street." The trader, whether he be corporation president or office boy in a small Western town, whether he work in a New York brokerage office or as a farmhand, becomes one of the "insiders" as soon as he has taken a semi-professional attitude toward the market, has mastered the rudiments of trading and digested the principles set forth in this volume.

The fact that he has done these things means that he is no longer buying and selling stocks "by ear" and in a casual way, as does the public, but that he is making a serious and studious attempt to make something out of stock trading beyond a hobby or an adventurous risk. To just the extent that he leaves this hit-or-miss method of trading and puts true research, analysis and system into his trading, any individual leaves the ranks of the so-called "public" and moves into the group of "insiders."

Both of these groups are so large and the terms so inclusive that there is no way of drawing very definite lines between them. It is only facing facts, however, to disillusion oneself and admit that the inside group is more successful in stock market trading, in the long run, than is the public. That is one of the economic tendencies that justify the writing of such a volume as this. And the reason why the insiders are more successful is not nearly so much because they have inside information as because they have made a science of trading rather than a casual hobby.

Granted, then, that the individual is interested in the stock market for some reason more potent than curiosity, he should study to place himself in this group of semi-professionals. He is doing just that as he reads these lines, but in more specific fashion he must constantly study the action of stocks to determine, if possible, what these insiders are doing. By joining forces with these governing factors he allies himself with them and increases his chances for profit.

Significance of Closing Prices

THERE IS ONE factor which is perhaps a little more important than much of the Wall Street credo. That is the significance and importance of the closing prices for stocks in general and the more active ones in particular. The active and best-known stocks are generally termed the "market leaders," and their course at any time determines in large measure the course of the "general market." During the five hours of regular trading on the stock exchange the "market" is generally moving either irregularly higher or lower. There are naturally many currents, but by and large there is usually detectable a fairly general tide, be it ebb or flow. The crowds which occupy the chairs in our leading commission houses are to be excused for their so-called indolence, for there is nothing more intriguing than to watch this ceaseless ebb and flow of stock market prices and to try to detect the first signs of faltering in one movement, which may presage the turning into the next counter movement. And, incidentally, while it is not at all necessary for mastering stock market trading, the watching and study of this true market action, right at the source, as it were, is splendid groundwork and a splendid school for the potential trader.

When one of these intermediate currents gets started in the course of a day's trading its own momentum carries it some distance. It may continue for many days with very little set-back but generally there are observable about anywhere from three to a half-dozen such definite alternating currents during a regular trading session. It is natural, therefore, to assume that if the market has lately developed a definite current just before the close of one day, that tendency will continue into the next day's session.

The importance of closing prices is a little stronger than just that, however, due perhaps in large measure to the fact that the public, as it reads the record of the day's trading in the evening papers that night, will judge the day as a whole and the prospects for the future largely by the closing prices rather than by the conflicting movements which have gone on during the earlier trading.

No matter what the definite reason, it is nevertheless true that if there is a well-defined movement on at the close, it is more than an even bet that the next day's market is to be a speedy one, for the closing movement usually carries on in greater strength and for a longer duration of time than the movements which develop and pass out again during the course of the usual day's trading. This is especially true if the previous movements of the day have been erratic, irregular and without any very strong trend. In such case, a strong upward movement at the close is almost sure to presage a good day tomorrow, or at least a good morning.

The exception appears in the practice of window dressing. It requires more experience than book knowledge or theory to differentiate between window dressing at the close of one day's trading, which is not genuine, and the genuine late-day trading movement, which augurs for higher prices tomorrow. The best clue which we can give here is that window dressing occurs generally before a longer holiday and not just overnight, and also the previous point that the late move is more likely to be genuine if it is a fairly strong move, if it reverses the general trend of the day or if it follows a day of high irregularity, without any particular trend predominating.

The Secondary Reaction

WALL STREET USUALLY expects that after a short recovery a "secondary reaction" will set in, due in part to scared traders who are merely waiting for a little recovery to sell out, and partly to the fact that stock acquired by banking interests for purposes of supporting the market and checking such a fast shake-out is merely for temporary holding and comes back on the market as soon as the decline has been checked. This secondary reaction may go a little lower than the first one, or it may not go quite so far. The latter picture is a much stronger one.

The secondary reaction was fairly dependable in years previous to the last two or three, but in these latter years there has been a tendency for the market to forget such a secondary reaction and to come back fairly steadily from an intermediate reaction. In any case, the best sign that the reaction is over is a further sharp dip in the morning, followed by sharp recovery in the afternoon with total volume of sales for the entire day at relatively high level.

When the major market movement is downward, indicating that a major bear market is in progress, then approximately the opposite rules hold. The major movement is generally indicated by the long-term trend, with the averages moving in the major direction quite steadily but also rather gradually. The intermediate reverses of the major movement are generally much sharper than the major movement itself. In a bull market, therefore, the reactions are short and sharp. In a bear market the recoveries are likewise short and sharp.

In a sharp recovery during a major bear movement, the secondary recovery is not so noticeable and is more likely to be entirely absent. Or at least what secondary recovery there is does not bring average prices back to the higher levels of the original recovery. The end of the recovery is also signalled, however, by sharp advance in the morning, followed by renewed decline in the afternoon and on relatively heavy trading for the entire day.

The Resistance Point

I N THE CASE of an intermediate reaction in a bull market the decline will quite often establish levels of support. A support level is a comparatively narrow price range, anywhere from one to ten points, below which the market, or the individual stock, does not appear disposed to move. A resistance level is a similar range above a stock which limits its advance. The formation of a resistance level or a support point may occupy almost any length of time, from one day to a year or more. The longer the time the level takes to form, the stronger is its indication that the next major movement will be in the opposite direction from that on which the support or resistance has been encountered.

The best picture in which is used the rule not to sell stocks short in a quiet market is when such support levels have been established after a sharp shake-out in a major upward movement. The market may hover near its low levels for a few days. If trading is still heavy, then it is quite possible that the reaction is not over. But if volume of trading shrinks gradually to lower levels with prices hovering irregularly about the support levels the chances are much more than even that the next movement will be a renewal of the upward trend.

When resistance levels are formed after an intermediate recovery in a major bear movement they are not nearly so dependable in indicating that the next move is to be downward, but they are still worthy of consideration. Likewise, the decline in trading at such time is also not so dependable but is likewise a fair indication that the buying power on the recovery has been expended and that the major downward trend is to be resumed.

Wall Street Formula

ONE OF THE "old rules" of Wall Street trading, especially in a bull market, is to "take your losses but let your profits run." It is hardly a rule and there is much to be said on both sides, but in general it is worthy of serious consideration. The theory is that if the trader gets into a stock that declines instead of advancing in a major bull market it cannot be a very good stock, there must be some hidden reason for its decline, that decline may well go further, and he is better out of it and into something that is acting better. One stubborn streak which leads a trader to hold on to a poorly acting stock may eventually wipe out the profits on many successful trades.

On the other hand, if the trader gets into a stock that is truly going up in a bull market a few points profit is not enough and there is no telling how high it may go. Thus he should "let his profits run." The most satisfactory method of limiting any losses to small proportions, of course, is to protect the purchase by a stop-loss order. Such orders must be placed after studying the normal past action of the individual stock, but they are generally set from three to six points below the purchase price. The trader therefore knows that if he is wrong he cannot lose more than the number of "points away" from the purchase where he has placed his stop order, whereas if the stock advances he is constantly accumulating paper profits.

The objections to the rule are that many a day in any bull market sees bear traders, "gunning for stop-loss orders." That is they take advantage of this trading rule and pick on one stock after another, which they strong-arm into a sharp decline. As the stock declines its lower prices catch the stop orders below the market, the automatic selling of these stocks depress the issue still further and the bear traders cover their short sales on this further decline. Thereafter, of course, since the dip was only technical and temporary, the stock rebounds, but the trader who had his stop-loss order caught has lost his position in perhaps a very good stock.

Buying at Support Levels

THERE IS ONE point which needs further treatment in connection with avoiding the disappointments of having stop orders caught in long purchases. This is the practice of buying only at support points, and it affords a much better background for the trading profit-or-loss formula than otherwise. We have previously seen that a resistance level on the up-side, or a support level on the down-side, is a comparatively narrow price range through which the stock, or the general market, does not seem disposed to go. We shall have more to say about such support and resistance levels when we are studying market action by charts, for it is there that resistance points are most easily observed.

It may be noted, however, that some stock has been tending generally upward but has lately had a reaction from its high of 100 to current levels of, say, 75. Suppose that the stock recovers to 90, reacts to 77, recovers to 85, reacts to 74, recovers to 80 and reacts to 75. The limit of the recoveries has not been regular but the limit of the declines has been confined to the support level of around

75. When such a support level is observed it presents a good opportunity to use the profit-or-loss formula. The stock may be bought at around 76, with a stop-loss order at 72. The formula may then be that the trader will either lose four points or win 10. He puts in a coupled order to "Sell at 86 or 72 stop. Coupled. G.T.C."

He may feel fairly sure that the stock will not sink below its support level. If it does he should be glad to be out of the stock, for it would not be a good sign. On the other hand, it is probable that if the stock does not go through its support level on the down-side it will advance to a point where he can accept his formula profit. Of course, if he can do this three times out of five he will make money. The principle of studying resistance points makes the profit-or-loss formula more valuable but it is still a bit too dangerous and automatic to be considered a consistent friend.

Of course, the support level may be used successfully in any type of trading. On theoretical principles, however, it would not be good policy to accept a smaller profit than the limit of possible loss, since the odds would then be definitely against the trader. But profits may be accepted at any time such action is wise in the trader's opinion. He may play for a five point profit or a 10, may use the progressive stop to protect profits or may merely take such profits when the advance seems to have gone far enough. Once more, the method of using one's own judgment rather than depending upon absolute formula is probably most satisfactory from the standpoint of the serious and semi-professional trader.

"Gaps" in Stock Charts

THE LAWS OF action and reaction account largely for still another technical chart tendency which is very often valuable, especially in short-turn trading. This is the use of formulae for covering gaps in chart trading. A chart gap or spread is a vertical gap, or open space, between one day's range and the next. It means that the low of one day is higher than the high of the previous day or that the high of one day is lower than the low of the previous day. This results in "open water" or a gap between the two days' ranges. It is easily seen that such a spread results from a sharp jump or drop in the price of a stock.

The theory is that sooner or later the stock will return and "cover" this spread or gap. Usually the spread is covered very soon, perhaps the next day. Sometimes it is not covered for months. In rather rare instances the spread is never covered and, as usual, the rule therefore has its exception. When the spread is not covered it is almost always followed by a very long and profitable major movement in the direction of the original spread.

The exception is very important, however, for it comes generally a a particular stage in the market formation and forecasts the beginning of a sharp, long and profitable movement in that direction. This ex ception is generally found after any of our seven cardinal formations indicating either a major advance or a major decline to follow. Perhaps the most common of these formations, as we have seen before, is the triangle. During the formation of such major pictures there may be many gaps, all of which will be subsequently covered as the major formation progresses toward completion.

As the triangle narrows down to a point, however, or we deduce from our previous experience with the seven major types that the formation of accumulation or distribution is coming to an end, we may begin to expect this exceptional gap formation which, unlike its broth- ers, is not to be covered. This type of gap constituted the "breaking away" from the previous formation which prophesied the coming move. Whether it be on the up or the down side, it is one of the best indications that the major formation is legitimate in forecasting a major movement and that such major movement has now begun.

It is the stamp of approval on the student's previous analysis of the preceding formation. It is only logical, therefore, to anticipate that since the looked-for movement is now under way, it will continue rapidly and strongly, and that this primary, or "break away" gap will not be covered, at least not for a good long time to come.

The other important type of gap is that which follows a long straight- away movement in either direction. This is the "exhaustion gap," which is almost a certain indication that the long and major movement is being exhausted and is near its end. This type of gap is almost always covered very shortly after it is made, for it indicates that the previous major movement is giving way to a reversal. Such reversal may be quite long and deep, often amounting to a more or less permanent reversal of the major move. It is a signal to switch to the opposite side of the market from the previous major move, and the fact that the forecasting gap of exhaustion is covered at an early date does not signify that the original direction will again be resumed, or nullify the general warning of further major reversal away from the previous movement.

We now have three chief types of gap. The first is the intermediate, or common gap, formed in ordinary trading, often during formation of one of our seven cardinal pictures, and almost always covered at no very distant future date. Due to the narrow swings accompanying such formations the trader will not make a great deal of money by playing for this common type of gap, though if he is agile, wide-awake, and wants to "scalp" the market, this common gap is almost infallible.

The second type of gap, we have seen, is the "break away" type. It follows the major formation, indicates the beginning of the major move previously forecast by the developing picture of accumulation or distribution, and is very seldom covered. It may be used best to check up on the correctness of the previous analysis, and as the final signal to get aboard for the profitable excursion.

The third type of gap, we have seen, is the "exhaustion" classification. It comes at the end of a long, swift and major movement, indicating the end of that movement and its major reversal. It is, therefore, almost the opposite of the break-away gap, which comes at the beginning of a long and profitable movement. The exhaustion gap is quite accurate and is a good signal that the previous major movement is near its end and that the trader's position should be switched in preparation for another major movement in the opposite direction within the near future.

All three types of gap may be found and used either in an advancing or a declining market, being equally profitable in each case. They are not 100 per cent reliable, but they are among the most accurate and reliable signals which the market student may discern in the study of charts.

The "New Era" Credo

FOR AT LEAST a year or two previous to the close of 1929 the cry from the house-tops was this familiar one that "we are in a new era." The laws of cycles, the laws of action and reaction, the basic fundamentals no longer applied because of the New Era—the golden age of American progress. Such statements are misleading because they are always at least partly true. Every period of business expansion or business depression is a new era. Times change and the world moves on. The recent period of prosperity, with the greatest bull market ever recorded in American history, was based upon many factors of a new era. But all the powers of science, of invention, of cost-cutting and labor-saving, of efficient management, co-operation and combination can hardly be expected to overrule the basic laws of supply and demand, of cyclical movements based on excess, and the fundamental theory that inflation in any line does not last forever.

The cry of a "New Era" is heard at the bottom of bear markets as well as the top of bull movements. In the former case it takes the form of argument that the "golden days are gone forever," that the nation's prosperity has passed its peak and that the cream is off of everything. The recent bull market was said to have resulted from a new American era due to our establishment as a creditor nation. The fact unquestionably had merit and served to prolong the bull market, but it did not mean that inflation could be continued indefinitely.

The United States was compared with Great Britain in her early flush of world leadership, but few of those who made the comparison took the time to study the past history of stock movements of that great nation. Unfortunately, the records are not very clear or continuous, but there is sufficient information to show that England went through numerous periods of inflation, based upon the same old cry in those days, of a "New Era" in British industry and world leadership.

HAROLD
M. GARTLEY

ster Market Technician

Harold M. Gartley is one of the illustrious names in the field of technical analysis, having laid the cornerstone for many of the basic concepts used by present day market technicians. His numerous articles and his book classic *Profits in the Stock Market* published in the 1930's are rare collector's items today, seldom seen and eagerly sought by all avid market students.

H. M. Gartley grew up in Newark, New Jersey where he attended the Newark Technical School, then went on to New York University, including the Graduate School where he received his Master's Degree in Business Administration as well as a Bachelor of Commercial Science Degree. He started in Wall Street in 1912 as a board boy and runner—progressed through back office, customers' broker, statistician, (now called security analyst), and finally to a partnership. He owned and conducted his own financial advisory and research organization from 1934 to 1947 with an exclusive clientele consisting of brokerage firms, banks, underwriters, law firms, and substantial investors. Today, Gartley is a Director of the National Securities and Research Corporation, one of the ten largest mutual funds. He is also one of the founders and a former member of the Executive Committee of the New York Society of Security Analysts. His life has been a busy one, including extensive lecture tours on the stock market in addition to conducting private courses for investors.

Since 1947, Gartley has been in the field of financial and shareholder public relations and has since become known as one of the outstanding authorities on the preparation of annual reports and other shareholder documents. He has been an Officer of the Public Relations Society of America, Inc., and today is Chairman of the public relations firm of Gartley & Associates, Inc., at 84 William Street, New York City.

Gartley's contribution to a *Treasury of Wall Street Wisdom*, his famous chapter on Trading Volume is from his famous classic *Profits in the Stock Market*, published and copyrighted by H. M. Gartley, Inc., 76 William Street, New York, a real landmark in technical theory and one of the very few extensive studies on the subject of volume ever published.

at a particular level. The reason for this is that, over long periods of time, the general level of activity so changes that it is not possible to select a permanent base from which to make observations for an indefinite period. Since S.E.C. regulation for instance (July, 1934), there has been a steady decrease in activity, but this has not changed the general implications of volume trends.

HISTORICAL CHARACTERISTICS

Anyone who reads the newspapers knows that in periods of prosperity stock markets are relatively active, while in periods of depression, they are relatively dull. In prosperous times, demand for stocks is stimulated by rising earnings and rising stock prices, and this demand grows increasingly effective as people have more savings available which they use for stock purchases. The supply to meet this demand increases readily enough from the strong boxes of the sophisticated holders, as they sell stocks to take profits and be out of issues which they believe are over-priced, and from corporations issuing additional shares as new flotations are offered to the public.

In periods of depression, volume of trading tends to diminish, because the trend of prices is downward, and the public is never attracted by falling prices. Activity in bear markets arises primarily from the force of liquidation, which starts with a tremendous burst of activity and continues, to a lessening but persistent degree, until the bear market is nearly ended. Early in a major downtrend, such as from November 1929 to April 1930, demand for stocks comes in fair volume from optimistic people who have money to "invest", but as successive waves of liquidation occur their optimism and pocketbooks are steadily depleted, until demand is very low. By that time the force of liquidation is spent, and the extreme dullness of a terminating bear market sets in.

VOLUME AND THE FOUR TRENDS

Let us first examine the record of volume in the four trends, the long term, major, intermediate and minor, and then endeavor to ascertain the usual characteristics of volume in the formation of some of the patterns which serve as working tools in technical study.

THE LONG TERM TREND

A study of the activity at bull market tops and bottoms from 1897 to 1932 indicates that the long term trend of volume was definitely upward in that period. The following table shows the average daily volume of trading at bear market bottoms and bull market tops from the bottom of 1897 to the major upward turn in July, 1932.

AVERAGE DAILY VOLUME

BEAR MARKET BOTTOMS		BULL MARKET TOPS	
Year	Volume	Year	Volume
1897	170,000	1899	500,000
1900	300,000	1901	1,000,000
1903	500,000	1906	1,600,000
1907	500,000	1909	2,000,000
1911	1,000,000	1912	700,000
1914	130,000	1916	1,850,000
1917	600,000	1919	1,700,000
1921	600,000	1923	1,200,000
1923	800,000	1929	4,000,000
1932	600,000		

It will be seen from the above Table that at bull market tops activity increased from an average daily volume of 500,000 in 1899 to an average of 4,000,000 in 1929, an increase of 700 per cent. At bear market bottoms, where public participation is always lacking, the average daily trading increased from 170,000 in 1897 to between 600,000 and 1,000,000 in later years, with the notable exception of the low of 130,000 in December of 1914, when the Stock Exchange was re-opened after a long suspension of trading.

From the Table it will be noted that with the exception of the 1911-1912 comparison, the average daily volume at the culmination of bull markets was several times that at the bottom of previous bear markets, showing that dullness characterizes the end of bear markets and the beginning of bull markets, whereas pronounced activity marks the end of bull markets and the beginning of bear markets. More will be said on this point presently.

The rising trend of volume from 1897 to 1934 is a reflection of the growth of the corporate form of business enterprise, increased public interest in such corporations, the great expansion in security holding effected by the war-time Liberty Loans, the tremendous growth in American industry and wealth, and the spread of stock trading activities to all classes in the latter years of the past decade. Whether S.E.C. regulation will level off this trend only time will tell. Most certainly the curbing of certain types of manipulation will (as long as it lasts) tend to flatten the long term upward trend of activity.

The long term trend of volume can be studied to best advantage on charts which are plotted on a monthly basis.

EFFECT OF REGULATION ON VOLUME

While this "mushrooming" public interest brought hitherto unheard-of activity and prosperity to the Stock Exchange community from 1926 to 1929, it might be said that Wall Street was then "sowing the wind" with little thought that some day it would "reap the whirlwind". When public interest was small, stock market debacles affected only the wealthier classes to any extent Rich Man's Panic of 1907, for example, and there was little outcry. But in 1929-1932, hundreds of thousands of citizens suffered financial paralysis, if not destruction, and others who did not lose directly blamed the depression on the much-publicized stock market. Strong public demand for regulation did not go unheeded by legislators, and while specific changes occasioned by regulation cannot be fully assessed at this writing, it is probable that in the future a repetition of the final stages of the feverish activity of the 1923-1929 bull market is less likely to occur.

If legislative restraints were not applied, the normal long-term trend of volume would no doubt continue upward, for, despite the ravages of the 1929-1932 bear market, trading in the advance of March-July 1933 was tremendous, and activity in May of that year broke all records for that month. But this was prior to the S.E.C.

MAJOR TRENDS

The sequence of volume characteristics in major trends may be summarized as follows:

Bull markets usually start out of the terminating dullness of the preceding bear market. The first intermediate upswing is accompanied by a **crescendo** of activity which continues through the culmination of the advance and the abrupt start of the intermediate correction. (See August and September, 1932, and April to July, 1933.) As the latter proceeds, however, volume diminishes and the correction normally terminates in dullness, from which the next intermediate advance starts (See October 1932, to February 1933). As the bull market progresses, each intermediate advance is apt to occur on bigger volume than the previous one (see 1923-1929). (However, this has not been the case since S.E.C. regulation in 1934. It will be noted that the January-February 1934, April 1936 and March 1937 tops occurred with the long term trend of volume decreasing.) Finally, a long period of heavy trading fails to produce a price rise worth mentioning, and a moderate decline occurs, with volume remaining active. This is the start of the ensuing bear market, as previously mentioned.

Summarizing, it is generally true that:

Bull markets usually begin in pronounced dullness, and end in prolonged, **intensive activity.** (We still have to learn whether or not S.E.C. regulation will permanently change this axiom.)

Bear markets naturally show the opposite tendency, and begin with a fairly moderate decline in prices wherein volume tends to increase instead of to decrease as in bull market price declines. As bearish characteristics develop, fear quickly grows to panic, and selling causes activity to rise to a point where daily trading for a time exceeds any seen in the preceding bull market. The selling climax of the panic produces a rally which shows a tendency to lose volume as prices advance.

Before very long, the major downtrend in prices is resumed, finally running into another selling climax. On this decline, volume increases again, but rarely equals that which appears in the first selling climax. This sequence continues through the bear market, with each climax showing somewhat less volume than the previous one, the tendency of activity to lessen being quite clearly marked.

In time, of course, the force of liquidation becomes spent. Demand, however, is light, because buying power is severely depleted and capital is timid. At this stage of the bear market, which is generally the final one, prices decline but activity is listless. Finally, activity becomes so light that the price trend flattens out and the bear market is about terminated as in July 1932.

Bear markets, therefore, show volume tendencies diametrically opposite to bull markets. They begin in great activity and end in pronounced dullness.

INTERMEDIATE TRENDS

Volume characteristics of intermediate cycles depend upon the prevailing major trend.

In Bull markets, the first major phase, as we have just seen, gains in activity as it progresses. However, volume does not reach a peak simultaneously with the price trend. Rather, the peaks of volume in the major phase usually occur during the mark-ups. At the actual top activity is heavy, but usually it is not as great as on the previous mark-up.

When the over-bought price structure collapses, daily volume rises until it often exceeds anything seen in the preceding major phase. This high volume is temporary, however, and as the corrective phase develops volume tends to dwindle, until dullness is pronounced at the termination of the corrective phase.

Thus, bull market **major phases** occur on **rising volume,** which frequently reaches a maximum on the last mark-up prior to the top. The **corrective phase** following starts in heavy trading, often heavier than any seen in the major phase, but this is soon supplanted by a **steady decline** in activity.

There were some variations in the major phases of the upward cycles of 1935 and 1936. We see that the largest activity between March 1935 and April 1936 was in May, during the first leg of the long rise. Subsequently, although there were periods of expansion, the high levels did not duplicate those of May. However, the characteristic of expanding volume during the markups of the major phase continued. New to bull market phases was the phenomenon shown in June-August 1935, and in March 1936, when activity tended to dwindle while prices advanced. As a matter of fact, the low level of activity during March was a factor which was regarded as quite bullish just prior to the sharp break in April.

In the 1936 rise from an extremely low level of activity in May, it will be noted that there was a steady expansion, although at no time did the total figures rise to levels comparable to those of 1932 and 1933, or for that matter even 1934.

Actually the activity in the 1936-1937 major phase was somewhat smaller than that in the previous 1935-1936 advance.

However, the tendency for volume to expand on markups and contract during price recessions continued as a normal factor. The fact that activity failed to expand to greater size in January of 1937 is an interesting commentary on the effectiveness of regulation in substituting a thin market with wide price fluctuations and low activity for a broad market with substantial activity. Normally at this stage in the 1936-1937 advance the volume in January should have made a peak for the move, such as let us say three or four consecutive days above 3,000,000 shares. The decline in activity in the March-June recession was typical of the corrective phase. It is interesting to note that in the previous correction in April 1936 there was practically no change in activity throughout this short period of three weeks, while prices had more than a 10% setback.

From this discussion we do not conclude that the characteristic volume sequence in a major phase of a bull market is greatly changed by S.E.C. regulation. But the fluctuations are certainly less pronounced, due to lesser activity.

In **bear markets,** the major phase of the first cycle is, of course, the decline which starts the bear market. (See September-November, 1929.) Activity is heavy and rises to a tremendous degree as the selling climax occurs.

The ensuing corrective phase (rally) begins from the climax, but loses activity as it progresses, until the advance practically "dries up" and a new major (downward) phase starts. This gains in velocity and activity as it descends until the selling climax is reached and the corrective rally occurs.

The corrective phase of the first downward cycle in the 1929-1932 bear market stands out as an exception to this general rule. In this case it will be noted that from January through early April, 1930, activity steadily increased.

On the other hand, notice how volume decreased from middle December 1930 to early February 1931. Here again we find an exception, in that activity picked up at the end of a corrective phase (February 7-27, 1931). During this sixteen-day false rally from the apex of the triangle, Wall Street gossip held that the bear market had ended with the December 1930 lows.

Thus, in bear markets, intermediate **major phases** occur on **rising activity** until their selling climaxes initiate **corrective phases.** Remember that there is **one exception**, namely, the major phase of the final bear cycle, wherein volume does **not** increase, but tends to dry up. The first major phase of a bull market, therefore, does **not** come out of heavy trading but out of dullness, and in this phrase volume does **not** dry up as in previous rallies in the bear market, but increases as the rally continues. This important technical factor contributed substantially to the author's shift from a bear to a bull market view early in August 1932.

In the study of intermediate trend volume, it must be understood that the trend of activity for a period of two or three months, or at least several weeks, must be surveyed as a whole. Conclusions concerning intermediate trend volume should not be drawn from the activity during a period of several days.

In the vast majority of cases, the trend of volume in individual issues will closely parallel the market as a whole during major and intermediate trends. On the other hand, there are numerous occasions wherein, for special reasons, the trend of volume over a period of two or three weeks in an individual stock will differ greatly from the market as a whole.

MINOR TREND

Minor trend volume, like minor trend fluctuations, is tricky and often difficult to analyze. For this purpose the trend of hourly volume is very helpful. Safe **general** rules to follow in observing minor trend phenomena are:

1. In **bull market major phases,** volume is more on the upward price movements than the declines, with trading light at the start, but increasing. **As the culmination of the major phase is reached,** volume spreads more evenly over up and down periods until **minor volume is less on rallies than on declines** and the correction begins.

2. In **bull market corrective phases,** volume usually appears on the

downside, but as the correction proceeds, activity lessens and minor trend volume tends to shift from declines to advances.

3. In **bear market major phases,** the tendency at first is only slightly toward increasing activity on declines, but as the price decline develops, volume appears more and more on the downside.

4. In **bear market corrective phases,** the early tendency is toward activity on strength, but as prices advance in the corrective phase, volume tends to grow lighter and occurs more on dips than on rallies.

Generally speaking, the first and last hours in each day are the most active, in all types of markets. This is because in the first half-hour the overnight accumulation of orders are executed, while in the last half-hour professional traders who try not to carry positions overnight "even up" before the closing bell.

HOURLY STUDIES OF MINOR TREND VOLUME

If the technical student desires to make a detailed study of volume, it is essential that intra-day activity be scrutinized constantly. The most convenient way to do this is to observe hourly volume. Since May 19, 1933, the New York Stock Exchange has published the total volume of trading hourly, which permits a more detailed study of volume for the market as a whole. Refined study, however, requires short interval volume data for individual stocks, and these data are not available at the present time unless they are compiled directly from the ticker tape. Such tabulations are extremely laborious. This is probably one important reason why volume research has lagged.

CAUTION

Students are warned that minor trend volume shifts rapidly and must be observed with skepticism. Remember that in minor declines during intermediate advances, volume may quickly develop bearish symptoms, but these can change to bullish indications with lightning rapidity. Conversely, during intermediate declines, volume may suddenly appear bullish, but just as quickly turn bearish. Minor trend volume on daily charts can be very deceptive, but it presents an even more difficult problem to the student who is going beyond daily figures and studying, say, hourly, half-hourly or twenty-minute volume figures. Analyzing volume minute by minute on a moving tape is a job for a veteran. However, with the proper background of experience, close study of this kind often permits early decisions at important turning points.

Before proceeding to a further study of volume characteristics, a discussion of sources of data, and some of the mechanical difficulties in plotting volume may be useful.

SOURCES OF DATA—PLOTTING VOLUME

Each day's individual stock volume is published in the larger metropolitan daily newspapers.

Hourly volume of trading is published on the New York Stock Exchange ticker tape, in *The Wall Street Journal* and other metropolitan dailies. It is very useful in studying the hourly averages. At present, there are no published sources of less than daily volume for individual stocks.

Customarily, chartists plot volume along the lower side of their charts. Some prefer to use bars, while others prefer a line type of plotting.

In studying total market volume many market students prefer to double Saturday volume, on the theory that it is a short day, and if volume is not doubled, meaningless valleys will occur at weekly intervals. Also, doubling volume on Saturdays tends logically to emphasize any substantial increase of activity during the short day.

There is a great difference of opinion as to whether volume should be studied on the ordinary arithmetic scale, or on the ratio, or semi-logarithmic, scale. Students favoring the arithmetic scale argue that the ratio scale, in compressing plotting figures in its higher ranges, just naturally defeats the easy study of volume, in that it is the volume peaks or sharp rises which are significant, and if they are compressed on the semi-logarithmic scale, it is a real handicap.

The other group who favor the semi-logarithmic scale, of which the author is emphatically one, present the counter argument that it is impossible to select a series of convenient arithmetic scales which will permit plotting of the wide ranges necessary in the study of a large number of individual stocks. Most chartists who use arithmetic scales for volume are in the habit of so changing the volume scales on their charts that only a few of the individual stocks they are studying may be compared one with the other. The use of the ratio scale eliminates this difficulty, and makes it possible to make accurate comparisons of the volume of any number of stocks, regardless of wide range in the statistics. Furthermore, the semi-logarithmic volume scale permits the study of volume ratios with the least effort in plotting.

VOLUME AND THE DOW THEORY

In outlining the seven precepts of the Dow Theory in Chapter VII, number six was volume. As outlined by Hamilton, it stated:

". . . When the market is oversold, activity goes dull on declines, and increases on rallies. When the market is overbought, activity goes dull on rallies and increases on declines."

All of the Dow Theorists constantly observe volume phenomena in connection with the other six tenets of the theory. When a previous high or low point is penetrated, they regard the penetration as more significant if it occurs accompanied by an increase in activity. The same is true when the price trend breaks away from either side of a Dow Theory "line". About two-thirds of the published conclusions of Rhea, Collins and Phelps, the contemporary writers concerning the Dow Theory, contain some mention of volume.

Dow Theorists look for volume to be at a high level at the culmination of bull markets, and at a low level at the termination of bear markets. Similarly they expect to see volume at a relatively high point at the end of major phases of intermediate cycles, and conversely at a low level at the end of corrective phases.

Charles Dow himself, in speaking of volume, said:

"In a bull market, dullness is generally followed by an advance; in a bear market, by a decline."

VOLUME AND THE OTHER WORKING TOOLS

In Chapters VIII-XIV, inclusive, frequent mention was made of the relation of volume to the other working tools. In each case, it was emphasized that as volume showed a marked increase in the direction of the trend, as indicated by other technical factors, it was a significant confirmatory signal worthy of note; while conversely, if volume failed to point in the same direction as the trend indicated by the other working tools, there was just reason to question the indications.

With some fear of repeating too much, let us now consider some general relations between volume and the other working tools:

VOLUME AND SUPPLY AND DEMAND AREAS

Briefly, a supply area forms when an advancing trend runs into more supply volume than it can absorb without losing headway. While there is sufficient demand volume to take all offerings, prices rise. When buying power wanes and selling becomes too persistent, either a trading area or a top forms.

Conversely, a demand area forms when a declining trend runs into more demand than is needed to absorb all offerings. As soon as sufficient demand appears to accomplish that, the downward direction of the price trend ceases, and a trading area or bottom forms.

Intermediate demand areas in a bull market are naturally at the end of corrective phases, when activity is at a relatively low level as compared with the previous top, for example. Conversely, the intermediate demand areas in a bear market are at the end of major phases, and in most cases activity is high, usually running into a selling climax.

Intermediate supply areas in a bull market are also at the end of major phases, and are usually accompanied by a substantial increase in activity, as compared with the intermediate low. Conversely, intermediate supply areas in a bear market appear at the tops of intermediate corrections, and are accompanied by less volume than was seen at the previous selling climax intermediate bottoms.

In some cases, there is a tendency for volume to expand during the corrective areas of intermediate cycles in a bear market. A good example of this appears in the period from October 1929 to April 1930.

The final supply area in a bull market, at the end of the last half-cycle, is usually accompanied by sustained activity during both diagonal and horizontal trends, while **the final half-cycle in a bear market** usually develops with activity at an extremely low level in both diagonal and horizontal trends.

As a general proposition, the volume characteristics of minor supply areas in both bull and bear markets, and in both major and corrective phases of intermediate cycles are all about the same. Minor tops in uptrends are usually accompanied by increased volume, and conversely in downtrends, by a drying up of activity.

Minor bottoms in uptrends are usually accompanied by a drying up of activity, and conversely in downtrends, by an increase in volume.

Occasionally, a minor bottom in an uptrend will be accompanied by a sharp increase in activity, as a bull market selling climax forms.

VOLUME AND TRIANGLES

Characteristically, **the triangle pattern is accompanied by a well-defined decrease in volume as it develops to its apex.** This is probably caused by the fact that the initial mark-up or mark-down which forms the third side of the triangle, being a dynamic movement, is accompanied by a sharp increase in volume, which sets up a peak. Then, as price fluctuations narrow down in the formation of the triangle, volume dwindles as uncertainty grows.

Of great importance is the fact that when the price movement breaks away from the apex of a well-defined triangle (remember that only well-marked cases are worth following), if the breakaway is accompanied by an increase in activity, it is less likely to be a false start than in the case of a rally or decline which develops in dullness.

It makes no difference which of the three types (ascending, descending or symmetrical) of triangle may develop—the declining volume characteristic is similar in all three, because it reflects the withdrawing from the market of persons interested in price fluctuations, because of growing uncertainty.

When **dynamite triangles,** covering a period of from three to five days develop, particularly in individual stocks, if there is a sharp step-up in activity early on the day when the price trend breaks away from the apex, it is a fairly reliable sign of a good buying or selling signal, according to the direction of the price trends.

VOLUME AND TREND LINES

When an important trend line is penetrated, it frequently happens that volume increases immediately after the penetration. It is likely that in recent years no small part of such volume arises from the activities of technical students who take positions promptly as the penetration occurs. When their guesses prove wrong, the volume soon dwindles and remains quiet. If their forecast is correct, volume continues at an active pace.

As most important trend lines, both intermediate and major, are penetrated during or by means of a mark-up or mark-down, it is to be expected that activity at such penetrations will increase as compared with that immediately preceding such an area. Where penetrations occur as a result of a sidewise movement, volume is likely to be notably small. Such penetrations are usually of doubtful significance.

Horizontal trend lines are usually penetrated on dull volume, with activity picking up if the move is important and continuing at a low level if the move is a false one.

VOLUME AND MOVING AVERAGES

In the penetration of moving averages applied to the price trend, particularly those used in connection with intermediate trend observation, a sharp step-up in volume is a sound confirmation of the importance of a penetration. As most of the more significant moving average penetrations occur as sharp mark-ups or sharp mark-downs, it is quite logical to see an increase in volume either coincident with the penetration, or a day or two following.

Volume phenomena in connection with the penetration of the minor trend moving averages are not sufficiently reliable to be very significant. There are many cases where a minor trend moving average is penetrated sharply for an hour or two, accompanied by an increase in hourly volume, which later prove to be false penetrations so that commitments made upon them prove unprofitable.

VOLUME AND GAPS

Experience shows that when an important gap occurs in the general price structure, as reflected in the composite and major group averages, volume increases sharply in the first hour's trading on that day. If the gap occurs at a point in the trend where a breakaway, measuring or exhaustion gap might be expected, its importance is emphasized if activity increases in the first hour. **If the price movement breaks out from a triangle wtih a gap and heavy volume, the move is likely to be even more significant.**

An upside breakaway gap is usually the point at which the notable increase in volume begins after trading has dwindled at a bottom. Upside measuring gaps more frequently than not appear in the price trend when volume has already increased substantially. Thus, they frequently occur without any notable increase in activity. Upside exhaustion gaps are almost always accompanied by a burst of volume which misleads the untrained observer to believe that the top is still much higher. As the exhaustion gap is usually part of the final mark-up formation, substantial trading is to be expected as it occurs.

The volume which accompanies the downside breakaway gap varies, and is not a dependable sign. In some declines, volume, already at a high level, increases sharply as the first part of the mark-down which follows a top gets under way. In other cases where downside gaps occur, activity slows down, giving a temporary bullish pattern. It is not until prices continue their decline that the volume increases to its characteristic peak in the reversal mark-down. Downside measuring and exhaustion gaps are almost always accompanied by a substantial increase in volume.

Before proceeding to a discussion of the refinements of volume studies, some emphasis should be directed to the phenomena of volume in connection with selling climaxes, which occur in both bull and bear markets but more often in bear markets.

To the trained technical student, the selling climax represents such an excellent opportunity to make stock market profits that it is important for the reader to be aware of the conditions which usually attend a selling climax.

SELLING CLIMAX BOTTOMS

The sequence of events in a selling climax, particularly in a bear market, is fairly consistent, and may be summarized as follows:

1. After the market has declined for some time, it closes at the bottom on a given day with ample evidence that the decline is not over. The news is preponderantly bearish, things look badly and appear to be getting worse, the "Street" is blue, customers' men suggest many specific reasons why prices should go lower.

2. On the next morning, there is a gap on the downside, substantial selling, prices fading away, thin bids, specialists with little on the "buy" side of their books.

3. On the tape—5,000 shares of this leader and that—possibly at substantial concessions, but often at only small concessions from previous prices. Frequently, reports come up from the floor indicating that one or more leading stocks, such as Steel, Chrysler, Telephone, or du Pont "are offered for a bid".

4. Then practically without warning, large blocks of the same stock are very much in demand, advancing half and full points, sometimes two points, between sales.

5. This advance often carries to the close, with no important setbacks and with heavy volume on the upside, quite contrary to its behavior in the preceding decline.

6. At the end of the day a study of the day's trading almost always shows an unmistakable sequence that confirms the intra-day phenomena.

These are the marks of a selling climax.

The last intermediate bottom at the end of the last half-cycle in a bear market is, of course, different from its predecessors in that it has bull market characteristics, chief of which is the tendency of volume to dry up on declines. Also, when fairly extended corrections (advances) are under way in bear markets, minor bottoms frequently occur on slackening volume, but these characteristics are counter to the underlying trend.

There is a real and difficult practical problem in connection with getting the most out of a selling climax, particularly for the average person who is interested in the market as a sideline, and thus finds the majority of his time engaged by his regular business. Briefly, the problem is this:

A selling climax is a phenomenon which often occurs in the course of two or three trading hours. The low prices are reached in hectic trading with markets in many stocks changing rapidly so that a bid or asked quotation of one moment is no good in the next.

The most advantageous purchases have to be made when selling has reached its peak, usually sometime in the first two hours of that day. Remember that the selling climax is an excellent example of mob psychology operating to its own discomfort. Because nearly everyone interested in stock prices is bearish at the same time on the morning of a selling climax day, bids are few and far between, and prices drop a half, one, or even two points between sales.

It is a matter of mere guesswork or chance if the average individual happens to pick a price somewhere near the bottom in the case of an individual stock during a selling climax. In most cases, open orders placed below the market do not offer a means of getting in at the right place, because it is anyone's guess as to where the panic of a selling climax will carry an individual stock level, before the recovery sets in.

In planning purchases in a selling climax, it is important that the trader keep clearly in mind that a point or two in the purchase price won't make much difference (except in low priced issues), because the rebound from the selling climax is likely to retrace one-third or one-half of the decline which preceded it. But this does not mean that a careful effort should not be made to make purchases somewhere near the bottom.

Probably one of the best methods available to the average trader is to assume that when prices have dropped sharply in the first two hours, and reports are coming up from the floor that leading stocks are offered for a bid, the time is ripe to make purchases.

Perhaps a peculiar experience which the author witnessed may help the reader to make some well-timed purchases in a future selling climax. When leaders were offered for a bid on the morning of a day which appeared as a possible selling climax day, orders placed one-half or one point above the last sale in two different selling climaxes in the 1929-1932 bear market obtained better executions than market orders for the same stocks, placed at the same time. It seems like an irrational procedure, but in a selling climax the bid and asked fluctuate so rapidly, that a buyer stands a far better chance of getting a good purchase price, when the selling climax is at its height, by being willing to pay up a little from the last sale. This margin provides the broker on the floor with a peculiar psychological stimulus which, in many actual cases in the past (believe it or not, Ripley), obtained mighty good executions.

Above, it was stated that there are selling climaxes in bull markets. These usually appear at the end of the corrective phase in a bull market cycle. They are not so pronounced as in the case of a bear market, because the force of liquidation is less acute, due to the fact that if the underlying major trend is upward the large bulk of stocks are being comfortably held for the long pull.

Nevertheless, the selling climax in a bull market provides one of the best opportunities for the stock trader to take his intermediate trend long positions. Worthwhile knowledge of these bull market selling climaxes may be obtained by studying the October 21, 1933 and July 26, 1934 reversals as well as the situations of April 28, May 13 and June 14, 1937.

There is no exact counterpart of the selling climax bottom, in the way of a buying climax top. Although it is true that many intermediate tops are accompanied by sustained activity at a high level, volume does not run up to a new high peak as it does in a selling climax bottom. There is no frenzied buying which compares with the panic selling during a selling climax. Probably this is because there is no force which makes people buy stocks, such as the relentless force of liquidation which often makes even the strongest holders sell their stocks in a bear market.

Usually, at the top of the major phase of an upward cycle, the trend of volume shows a tendency to flatten out, even though it is at a high level, as prices show a stubbornness to move forward any further. For example, look at the July 1933 top. In the case of the high points in April 1936 and March 1937, we see a definite tendency for volume to decrease preceding the high point. This definite decrease in activity prior to these two intermediate high points in the current bull market was a factor which threw many technical students off the track in judging the nearness of an intermediate correction. It still remains to be determined as to whether S.E.C. regulation, in reducing total volume of trading, has changed the typical high level of volume which usually exists in the several weeks prior to the beginning of a bull market intermediate correction.

VOLUME OF THE MAJOR AND MINOR GROUPS

Some students attempt to divide the study of total volume, and make observations of the aggregate daily and weekly volume in various groups of stocks, such as the Dow Jones 30 Industrials, 20 Rails and 20 Utilities. Others further subdivide the study of volume by observing the volume figures for minor groups, such for example the Herald-Tribune average of 15 Manufacturing, 10 Oils, or 6 Steel Stocks et cetera, for which the daily figures are published.

Although the author has made very comprehensive price studies concerning minor groups, no equally complete studies of minor group volume have as yet been attempted, because of the voluminous computations necessary in making a comprehensive survey of group volume for a sufficient period of time to provide worthwhile conclusions. Those readers who may desire to conduct a broad research program might well focus their attention toward the study of minor group volume, particularly by means of volume ratios, about which we will learn more later.

A study of group volume of the major and minor groups is undoubtedly useful, in that it contributes more detailed data with which to apply the premises suggested above. But it is the author's considered opinion that unless one has ample time, the study involves more work than it is worth, particularly because numerous experiments have shown that unless major and minor group volume figures are reduced to some standard, by means of ratios or logarithms, their value is decidedly limited.

REFINED AND MORE ADVANCED STUDIES OF VOLUME

Up to this point, all of our considerations of the volume of trading in shares of stock may be designated as studies, conclusions and premises based upon the statistics "in the raw". As many market students become more experienced, they soon find that the wide fluctuations in volume figures tend to confuse volume studies, to such an extent that precise conclusions are quite impossible.

Among the numerous methods which have been employed by statisticians and stock market students, for the purpose of eliminating the difficulties which arise as the result of these fluctuations, those which have come to the attention of the author may be classified in four general categories, as follows:

1. **Moving Averages of Volume,** wherein fluctuations in activity are smoothed out, in order to observe their trends more closely. Chiefly, these studies have been with 5-10 day moving averages of daily volume and 4-6 week moving averages of weekly volume.
2. **Volume Ratios,** wherein daily and weekly volume figures for individual stocks are expressed as percentages of the total trading in the market, and studied in these terms.
3. **Correlations of Volume and Price,** wherein the two phenomena are in some way combined to make related observations. The methods used in doing this are numerous, with the observations quite varied. Some are simple; others very intricate. In some cases

price and volume are multiplied while in others volume is divided by price or price change.
4. **Special Group Studies,** wherein the volume of investment stocks
and/or speculative stocks is studied in relation to the total trading.

MOVING AVERAGE OF VOLUME

Following the publication of hourly volume figures by the Stock Exchange in May 1933, technical students began to make hourly comparisons of activity in order to supplement their daily studies. The fluctuations in hourly volume were found to be so wide however anywhere from 40,000 to 3,320,000 shares; the range from January 2, 1936
to July 31, 1937 was between 40,000 and 1,020,000, the latter figure
being reached on March 3, 1937, that some method was necessary to
smooth out the rapidly moving curve. Naturally, the moving average was the first instrument employed. Because daily studies of volume
were so commonly used, a five-hour (one-day) moving average was
adopted by the author.

On *Chart 13** is a 5-hour **moving average** of hourly volume used with
the 15-stock aggregate plotted at 20-minute intervals. This 5-hour moving average is obtained by adding the volume for five consecutive
hours and dividing by 5. When a new hourly figure is available, the
earliest figure in the previous five figures is dropped and the new one
added, the total is again divided by 5 and so on. The plotting is made
at the end of the 5-hour period.

Moving averages of volume show a smoothed curve of the trend of
activity and permit more trustworthy identification of volume trends.
This smoothed curve shows an even distribution of the day's volume.
When the actual volume line appears above or below the moving
average line, the resulting peaks of valleys are considered relatively
more significant than during the periods when volume and its 5-hour
moving average are much alike.

*This refers to a chart that is no longer available.

If a substantial peak above the moving average accompanies a price advance, it is reasonable to assume that important progress is being made through substantial resistance, and further gains are indicated. If on the other hand a peak accompanies a decline, increased supply is indicated, and a further recession may be expected.

Conversely, if a peak forms and prices strike supply and fail to progress despite excessive volume, a top may be forming. Or if a price decline is checked despite a volume peak, demand is indicated and a bottom may be forming. It is suggested that this method be observed at great length before commitments are based upon it. Decidedly, it is a minor trend study for the advanced student.

VOLUME RATIOS

As the stock market student progresses in his learning, he finds that relative figures are almost always more useful than raw data (actual figures). The more advanced observers thus study not only actual volume of trading in a stock for a given period, but also the ratio or per cent which that volume represents of the total volume of trading. If both series are plotted on the same scale, it is advantageous to use lines rather than bars, although some chartists prefer to use bars for the actual volume and a line for the volume ratio, both plotted on the same scale. **(The study of volume ratios applies specifically to individual stock observation.)**

WHY VOLUME RATIOS ARE IMPORTANT

Let us illustrate the reasoning why volume ratios are a necessary refinement in the study of individual stock volume by considering the simple tabulation which follows:

CHRYSLER	TOTAL MARKET VOLUME	PER CENT OF TOTAL VOLUME (VOLUME RATIO)
150,000	1,500,000	10.0
100,000	1,000,000	10.0
150,000	1,000,000	15.0

If 150,000 shares of Chrysler are traded on a particular day when the total market volume is 1,500,000, the ratio would be 150,000/1,500,-000, or .10, meaning that the trading in Chrysler was 10 per cent of the total trading on that day.

If, on the next day 100,000 shares of Chrysler were traded, and the total market volume decreased to 1,000,000 shares, the activity in Chrysler would still be 10 per cent, and there would be no relative change in the activity in Chrysler, notwithstanding the fact that there had been an actual change from 150,000 to 100,000 shares, or a decrease of 33$\frac{1}{3}$ per cent. As the total volume in the market was decreased by the same amount, there was not a relative change in Chrysler activity. It merely followed the market.

But if, on the other hand, on the third day the trading in Chrysler totaled 150,000 while the total volume remained at 1,000,000 the percentage of trading in Chrysler would have advanced from 10 per cent to 15 per cent, or an increase of 50 per cent over the previous day. This would be construed as very significant, because the trading in Chrysler would have been relatively **more active,** while the total trading **remained the same.**

The value of volume ratios lies in the fact that they show the relative trend of volume. To the uninformed observer, an increase in the volume of trading looks significant, regardless of whether it is in line with the fluctuation apparent in the market as a whole. To the trained observer, volume is significant only when it shows a change in relation to the total volume.

The study of relative volume by means of ratios (percentages of total volume) is particularly important when a noticeable peak or valley or trend in the ratio is apparent coincident with some other technical factor, which may be confirmed or denied by the action of volume—for example, a breakaway from a triangle, the penetration of a trend line, or the breaking of a previous high or low point.

A study of several hundred volume ratios, over a period of several years, clearly shows that there is no significant peak in actual volume which does not show up in relative volume (the ratio to the total trading). On the other hand, there are numerous occasions where a notable increase or decrease is not discernible in the raw figures, which is clearly apparent in the relative figures. That is, there are many occasions where the raw figures show nothing significant, while the ratio figures develop important indications; but there are no occasions where a significant indication shows itself in the raw figures which is not equally apparent in the refined data.

If this writer had his choice of watching charts of the actual volume figures, or charts showing the ratio of volume figures, he would select the ratios and drop the actual figures, unless trading operations were large enough to require a knowledge of the actual number of shares traded. Some of the corporate investors and very large individual investors of necessity must follow the actual figures in order to plan their accumulation and distribution because the number of shares they buy and sell is large enough to influence the market. The same is true of some of the large investment counsel organizations.

One of the advantages of using volume ratios instead of the actual figures for volume is that they can be plotted on arithmetic charts without any of the difficulties of changing arithmetic scales. Ordinarily, the daily trading in the 700-800 most active stocks varies in the range from about .05 per cent to 10 per cent. Although this range at first seems very wide, it is relatively small compared with the range of actual figures, which vary from 100 shares to 300,000—400,000 shares a day.

ONE GREAT VALUE OF VOLUME RATIOS

Perhaps the greatest value, however, in studying volume ratios ver-

sus the raw figures is that when they develop a peak comparable to the highest two or three peaks in the previous year or two, an important development in the price trend is almost always under way; whereas in the raw figures, numerous peaks which appear to the eye as possibly important are of no significance whatsoever.

Usually, in the course of 18 months, in a fairly active stock there will only be three or four important peaks in a volume ratio; 7 out of 10 such peaks will be signals of importance to the technical student whereas during the same time period, 15 or 20 peaks, of which only a third or a half later prove to be of importance, will develop in the actual volume line.

PRICE-VOLUME CORRELATION
PRICE-VOLUME STUDIES—CORRELATION
OF VOLUME AND PRICE

The discussion from this point to where the summary begins is presented for those readers who are interested in some of the research developments in price-volume relations, being employed by more advanced students. The vast majority of the studies in this category require considerable labor in their preparation, and unless they are used in connection with the operation of a large trading fund, they are hardly worth the effort involved.

THE EARLIEST PRICE-VOLUME CHART

For years market students have toyed with the idea that a given amount of advance or decline in price could be measured in terms of turnover or volume. The premise usually adopted is that in an advance, for example, if for each one point of rise 10,000 shares are traded, supply is being encountered as soon as 20,000-30,000 shares are traded with a rise of only one point or less. At first this system of measurement

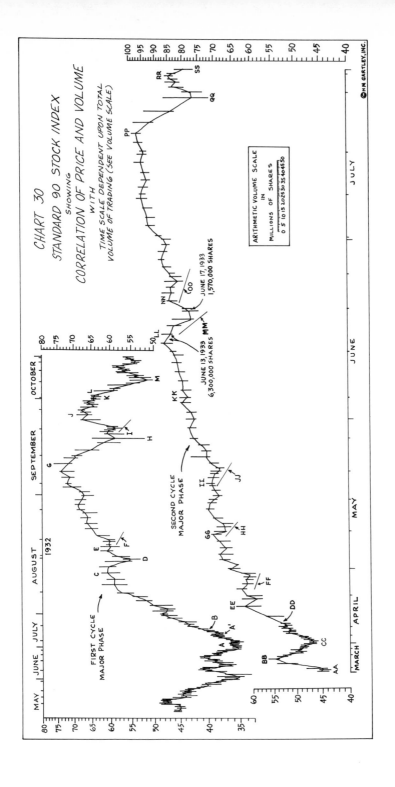

CHART 30
STANDARD 90 STOCK INDEX
SHOWING
CORRELATION OF PRICE AND VOLUME
WITH
TIME SCALE DEPENDENT UPON TOTAL
VOLUME OF TRADING (SEE VOLUME SCALE)

ARITHMETIC VOLUME SCALE
IN
MILLIONS OF SHARES
0 5 10 15 20 25 30 35 40 45 50

© H.M. GARTLEY, INC.

FIRST CYCLE
MAJOR PHASE

SECOND CYCLE
MAJOR PHASE

JUNE 13, 1933
6,300,000 SHARES

JUNE 17, 1933
1,570,000 SHARES

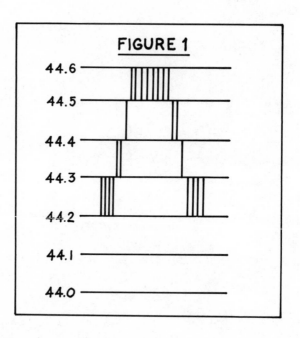

FIGURE 1

appears very logical, simple and direct. But when it is studied for a while, it is quickly found that there are many occasions where the method falls down badly and causes many losses if used alone in actual trading.

Essentially, most of the price-volume studies are devices which have -grown out of an old type of bar chart used before 1900 by tape-readers. If a trader were operating then in Steel, he would watch the tape for all the shares traded in the stock. When a sale of 100 shares came out, at 44.2, he drew a vertical line at the 44.2 level on his chart, as illustrated in Figure 1. If the next sale was 300 shares at the same price, he drew three more lines at the 44.2 level. Following this, let us say, 200 shares of Steel sold at 44.3, 100 at 44.4, and 500 at 44.5. The trader then drew two lines at the 44.3 level, one line at the 44.4, and five lines at 44.5 as shown.

Three more sales of 100 shares each were then made at 44.5; 100, 100 at 44.4; 100 at 44.3; 300, 100 at 44.2. For each 100 shares sold, the trader drew a line at the appropriate price level, securing the graph illustrated. This type of chart enabled the trader to recognize important supply and demand areas by the volume which occurred at such levels. In the example cited here, Steel was obviously in supply at 44.5.

THE PRINCIPLE APPLIED TO THE STANDARD 90 STOCK INDEX

An interesting example of graphic correlation of price change and volume is given on *Chart 30.* The series in the upper left-hand corner shows high, low and closing prices (closing prices connected by continuous line) for the Standard Statistics 90-stock average from May to October, 1932. This period covers the bear market low, the major phase of the first intermediate cycle, and the early part of the correction of this major phase. The lower series shows the major phase of the second intermediate cycle, from March to July 1933. Both series are plotted on the same ratio price scale.

TIME SCALE BASED ON VOLUME

The reader will immediately note that, unlike the usual high, low and last bar chart, the bar plottings on *Chart 30* appear at unequal intervals on the time scale.

This is because the bars were spaced in relation to volume rather than to predetermined horizontal time units, customarily standing for a day. The usual spacing assigned to a time unit was given to the unit of 1,000,000 shares of total activity, as indicated on the Arithmetic Volume scale shown at the lower right-hand side of the Chart. On June 13, 1933, for example, 6,300,000 shares were sold. The high, low and last bar for this day is plotted, not one unit of horizontal distance to the right of the bar representing the price range for June 12, as in ordinary daily interval bar plotting, but 6.3 units of horizontal space, representing 6.3 millions of shares of volume. In the same way, the volume on June 17 was 1,570,000 shares. The high, low and last bar for that day is plotted 1.57 units of horizontal space to the right of the bar standing for June 16. The plotting thus combines price and trading activity in one series.

INTERPRETATION OF CHART 30

In order to interpret *Chart 30,* it is necessary to recall the following axioms about volume, stated in somewhat different phraseology than in the early part of this Chapter:

1. When prices are **rising** and volume is **increasing,** the advance is impressive. Conversely, if prices are **rising** and volume is **decreasing,** the advance is questionable.
2. When prices are **falling,** and volume is **increasing,** the decline is impressive. Conversely, when prices are **falling** and volume is **decreasing,** the decline is questionable.
3. If an advance halts, or if little progress is made on the up-side, with activity **large,** a possible **top** is signaled.

4. If a decline halts, or if little progress is made on the down-side, with activity large, a possible **bottom** is signaled.

All experienced students view the market with these axioms in mind. With the customary chart showing daily price range in one series and volume in another at the bottom of the chart, it is necessary to correlate the two series with the eye, in order to apply these volume axioms. In *Chart 30*, however, both price and volume phenomena are graphed in one series.

In July 1932, at the bottom of the bear market, it will be noted that stocks traded in a narrow range or Dow Theory "line" (A) on very light volume, denoted by the close spacing between the bars. Shortly after this line was broken on the up-side, volume picked up (the spaces widened), giving evidence that the breakout was probably important. A slight recession occurred between A and B and volume declined, giving a bullish signal (the spacing between the bars contracted again at A^1). This was confirmed following B, when activity increased on the sharp mark-up (spacings expanded). Throughout the mark-up from A to C, volume continued to expand. At C, volume was very large, and little progress was made on the up-side, indicating the nearby possibility of a reversal.

On the decline from C to D, however, volume tended to dry up, suggesting the end of a reaction. When prices rebounded to E, volume again picked up, but decreased on the set-back to F, once more signalling strength. From F to G volume continued heavy, but the price gain was smaller proportionate to that made from A to E.

The increased space between the high and low bars, together with the slowing up of the advance, clearly indicated that the market was running into supply. At G, activity was extremely great, with no price gains, and the forecast correction to H on high volume followed. After the bottom at H had formed, volume decreased on the small reaction which took place at I. This bullish indication was confirmed by an expansion of volume on the rally to J. Further confirmation developed as activity dwindled from J to K, but the down-side break at L on high volume abruptly reversed this bullish signal, and gave indications that the corrective phase was to continue. At M, volume again tended to dry up, suggesting the possibility that the corrective phase was over.

From M on the upper series to AA on the lower series, there occurred a long trading area on relatively light volume. Volume signals during this period were relatively unimportant.

In the lower series, after the formation of the low at AA in March 1933, activity increased sharply on the advance to BB following the Bank Holiday. This increase compares with point B in the upper series, except that in the lower series the expansion of volume was pronounced. On the decline from the top at BB to CC, activity dwindled, denoting strength. The rally from CC was marked with a gradual increase in volume until the previous high (BB) was approached at DD, when volume expanded sharply on the upward penetration to give an important buying signal. The decline in volume on the small reactions from EE to FF confirmed the signal, and additional bullish evidence was furnished by the tendency of volume to dry up on the declines from GG to HH and II to JJ.

From JJ to KK, volume expanded on the rally, but from KK to LL the advance slowed up on increasing volume, indicating the possibility of a nearby reaction. The high volume from LL to MM was decidedly bearish, for, unlike the previous reactions to CC, FF, HH and JJ, activity increased on the decline. Subsequently, however, volume again increased on the rally to NN, and declined slightly on the reaction to OO, giving bullish indications which were justified by the advance from OO. As the top PP was reached, high volume continued with virtually no price gains, and the market broke sharply to QQ on an avalanche of selling. This situation compares with that in the upper series from G to H, in September 1932. On the rebound from QQ to RR, volume declined, continuing the bearish indication.

Thus, on *Chart 30,* which combines price movement and activity in one series, we are able to see fairly consistent phenomena from which deductions as to important market reversals can be made.

In the period from June 1933 to August 1937, covering practically four years, during which two complete bull market cycles made their appearance, the volume characteristics shown on *Chart 30* were not duplicated, although a study of the previous 36 years shows that the phenomena covering the period 1932 and 1933 were repeated time and again.

It is this author's opinion that as long as S.E.C. regulation controls manipulation comparably to the period 1935-1937, it is possible that a study like that shown on *Chart 30* will be of small value.

TRENDOGRAPHS—A FURTHER REFINEMENT

Figures 2-6 inclusive show a further development of a price-volume correlation study. They illustrate what is probably the greatest current development of graphic correlation of price and volume, and show the work of Mr. E. S. Quinn, Vice-President of Investographs, Inc.* Trendographs, Inc., a division of Investographs, Inc., publishes a series of 60 such charts which are issued weekly. The reproductions were furnished and presented with the permission of Mr. Quinn.

The studies which Quinn has made of price-volume correlations of individual stocks are employed as part of a comprehensive program of studying volume in the market as a whole. He begins with consideration of the relation of volume in certain investment and speculative groups, for the purpose of determining what we have termed the "When" to buy or sell question. He then carries the study through a process of examining the individual volume characteristics, both actual and relative, of a picked group of stocks, to the point where the price-volume relation of these stocks is made the basis of answering the "What" question.

But let Mr. Quinn tell his own story, in the following quotations which he has kindly furnished the author.

*31 Gibbs Street, Rochester, New York

QUINN'S GENERAL PHILOSOPHY

"Trendograph procedure is founded upon the proposition that rising prices follow investment buying of values; that declines are caused by gambling in intangibles.

"Whenever the sales price of an article in general demand descends to the point where a sufficient number of prospective purchasers recognize its **fundamental, economic** value and would rather own the article than the cash required to buy it, it will not go lower. This reasoning holds whether the article in question is real estate, commodities, stocks or anything else. But there is a significant distinction here which should be understood. It is economic values which provide a base—**not** speculative possibilities.

"Similarly, whenever the price of an article exceeds its fundamental value, either on the basis of reproduction cost or intrinsic investment or economic value, its market position is weak and its price cannot be long maintained.

"A familiar practical example is represented in the Florida land boom of some years ago. Before prices started to rise so spectacularly, properties could be acquired at figures reasonably close to basic values and, just so long as the spread between prices and values was small, the land situation was sound.

"As Florida became a fad, however, and prices sky-rocketed far beyond the levels of values, it was impossible to secure adequate returns on land investments. People were buying properties not because they wanted to keep them, but solely in the hope of selling out to someone else for more money than they paid. Financing loans could not be supported and it was only a question of time before the inevitable collapse occurred.

"Other well known instances include the unsuccessful attempt of Brazil to hold the price of coffee at levels which were economically unsound and Britain's effort to peg the price of rubber, both of which brought disastrous results. Another example, equally doomed to failure, is the program our Government is carrying on currently in trying to maintain the price of cotton above world market values.

"When a general market decline is in progress, it will continue, irrespective of previously held conceptions of values, until prices reach the point where they represent values at that time, under the new conditions which then prevail. When a sufficient number of interested persons recognize the existence of sound values, prices will not decline further because such offerings as are made will be absorbed, so that the trend will be reversed and prices will rise. The natural question here is: 'How can one know with reasonable accuracy when stock prices are forming a "value" base?' The answer to this is found in analysis of the character of general trading, which discloses whether stocks are largely being purchased for value or for speculation.

"We know that the point has been reached where true values are being recognized, when value stock, such as American Telephone, Union Carbide, Allied Chemical, Woolworth and others like them, are being bought. Their purchase is not being stimulated because of their speculative appeal because, normally, they are slow movers and, percentagewise, gain less than the market as a whole in a general advance. They are being acquired because, at current yields and according to balance sheet values, they are worth more than the cash required to purchase them. Moreover, as a class, the individuals who buy these stocks are not speculatively inclined in the sense that they do not make their purchases on borrowed money. They pay outright for their shares. Such purchases at such times are economically right and supply the force which stops market declines.

"Concentration of trading in investment stocks means that there has been a proportionate shrinkage of transactions in speculative shares. Lack of offerings in the latter classification is evidence that such necessitous liquidation as may have been overhanging the market, as the decline originally got under way, has been completed; that accounts which were vulnerable have either been sold out or strengthened. Obviously, when speculative holdings are no longer being pressed for sale and there is an active demand for investment stocks, the market is basically healthy and prices will not go lower.

"After the market has formed a base and starts to rise, it will continue its forward move until prices run too far ahead of intrinsic values, whereupon it will fall of its own weight. Here, too, we recognize the approach to a turning point by analyzing the relationship between investment and speculative trading in the market as a whole.

"As the market moves ahead, investment stocks become less attractive, so that the demand for them begins to taper off. And this demand becomes proportionately less as prices move further away from values. Somewhere in this phase the small gamblers start coming in, attracted by the gains they have been watching from day to day. Their number is legion—and their lack of knowledge of market affairs is nearly as great. Their combined purchases carry prices still higher. But while they are buying, so-called wise money is being withdrawn. Soon the stock market loses its character as a common ground for the exchange of values for currency. It becomes a meeting place for gamblers, big and little, whose purchases are largely made on borrowed money, purely in the hope of quick, easy profits. Such purchases, because of their temporary nature, constitute a constant threat to the health of the market as a whole because, on the first sign of serious price-weakness, dumping begins. As the decline continues, it compels added selling for the protection of margins and thus feeds on itself until weakly-held accounts are cleaned up and prices reach the point where values establish a new base.

"These are the economic principles used in measuring the degree of underlying strength or weakness of the market. The actual selection of stocks to be used is made from observation of the performance of individual issues.

PRICE-VOLUME FACTORS MUST BE RELATIVE

"The proper analysis of the operation of the law of supply and demand within individual stocks serves two essential purposes. Not only does it reveal the trend of public interest; it also discloses whether such interest is favorable or unfavorable. In Trendograph charts, a study of supply and demand is employed as a means of showing the trend and character of public interest in the various stocks.

"The volume of trading in any particular stock will normally represent a certain percentage of the volume of trading in the market as a whole. This is an axiom which many chartists, who base their conclusions upon absolute volume, have entirely overlooked. Seeing volume in a stock increase substantially, they look for some reason to buy or sell, not realizing that if general volume has increased in proportion, the situation is of no significance.

"Obviously, a stock which merely drifts along, consuming only its normal volume of trading from day to day, is without particular public or private interest and for this reason does not offer good trading prospects. But when any stock shows a large increase in relative volume; when it suddenly begins to consume more than its usual percentage of total trading, only one conclusion can be drawn. Some individual or group has decided—and their judgment is being backed up by their own cash—that the stock is selling either too high or too low.

"This leads to two conclusions. First, **that it is impossible to interpret the meaning of volume fluctuations in a stock unless these are tied up percentagewise with total market volume.**

"Second—and this is important—**the percentage relationship provides a means of recognizing instantly any unusual activity in a stock.** Whether such unusual activity is buying or selling may be determined by considering the coincident price action.

"Just as volume in a single stock must be considered in relation to total trading, price movements of individual stocks are misleading except as they are compared with the trend of the market as a whole.

287

Simply because a stock may gain 2% in value in a day is not necessarily favorable—It is if the market as a whole gained 1%. It is not if the market as a whole has gained 3%. Similarly, it is not necessarily unfavorable if a stock declines 2% on a given day. If the market at the same time lost 5%, then the stock is showing strength merely in resisting the general decline.

CONSTRUCTION OF THE TRENDOGRAPH CHARTS

"In a standard Trendograph chart (see Figures 2-6 inclusive) the upper rectangles coordinate daily price ranges, vertically, and relative volume, horizontally. Wide rectangles mean greater relative volume; narrow ones, less. Since relative volume is the interest-indicator, we look for any sudden broadening out in the horizontal dimensions of the rectangles. If, on increased activity, a stock moves ahead of the market, a plain indication is given that the demand for that stock is greater than the supply as compared with the relationship of these forces in the market as a whole. This, under certain conditions, would be interpreted as a buying signal, particularly if underlying conditions in the general market are favorable.

"To permit direct comparison of relative price movements, two connected, irregular lines are superimposed upon the pattern of the price-volume chart of the stock. The heavy line is the general market as represented by the daily changes in the sum of the three Dow Jones averages—Industrials, Railroads and Utilities. This combined average provides the basis upon which all relative price movements in individual stocks are computed. The lighter, broken line gives the trend of average stock prices in the specific industrial group classifications (such as Agricultural Implements, Chemicals, etc.), to which each stock is assigned. Accordingly, it is possible at a glance to analyze price action in any given stock, both with respect to the general market and its particular group.

"The supplementary chart is really more important than the price-volume curve which it supports. The zero line represents the market 'straightened out'. The black vertical bars, extending both upward and downward from it, provide a breakdown of the daily price action of the stock in comparison with the price action of the market as a whole. The vertical distance of a bar above the line shows the percentage by which the price of the stock exceeded the averages on a given day; comparative losses are reflected below the line. The width of these bars indicates relative volume.

"The cross-hatched (shaded) areas between the vertical lines, marking calendar weeks, show the net percentage gains and losses of the stock, by weeks, in excess of the market.

"In practical use, it will be found that the upper section of the Trendograph chart is valuable principally as a means of gaining an accurate perspective of both near term and long term price habits and volume characteristics. Obviously, if a particular stock displays a constant repetition of price-volume habits throughout rallies and declines and at tops and bottoms, a knowledge of these factors is most useful in predicting what the future might bring.

"The lower section of the chart form provides a detailed breakdown of comparative action, which is another way of saying a representation of the daily operation of supply and demand. This section of the chart is used in analyzing current action in order to determine whether or not the underlying condition of a stock is strong or weak.

VOLUME HABITS OF STOCKS AT TOPS AND BOTTOMS

"Stocks are like people in that they have varying and, in many cases, definitely established habits. It is for this reason that Trendograph charts going back to January 1932 have been prepared. By studying these, one is able to recognize what a given stock normally does at tops and bottoms and in rallies and declines, and is thus in a position to attempt a forecast of future action which is almost certain to be more accurate than if this knowledge were not available.

"As has already been explained, the general market forms a base under pressure of investment buying; tops are seen to the accompaniment of gambling in intangible speculations. In the practical use of Trendograph procedure, analysis of the current position of a stock usually begins with consideration of its relative-volume characteristics at tops and bottoms.

"Accordingly, in an investment stock, we recognize the approach to a base and a buying level, while market prices are still declining, when we see our charted rectangles begin to expand horizontally, evidencing increased investment demand. Once a purchase has been made, we watch volume as the general market moves ahead. When volume begins to shrink, we know we must begin to think about selling, because the operation of the law of supply and demand is telling us that intrinsic value has become questionable. Re-purchases of investment stocks are not made until relative activity again broadens out after a decline. Trendograph charts of many investment stocks over a period of years show that American Can, American Telephone, du Pont, U. S. Steel, Union Pacific and others display a surprising consistency in volume characteristics. Relative volume expands as such stocks approach buying areas and narrows down at tops.

"In similar fashion, we follow the general swings in a speculative stock, except that the opposite interpretation applies. The approach to a buying point can be seen as volume dries up, indicating a lack of selling pressure. A purchase is made as soon as price action shows the stock to be in a position to rise. As our stock advances, again we watch volume, but this time we look for increased activity as an indication of the probable termination of the advance and get ready to sell. Striking examples of small volume bottoms and large volume tops are seen in Trendograph charts of Columbia Gas & Electric, Douglas Aircraft, Electric Bond & Share, Montgomery Ward, U. S. Smelting and others.

"While up to this point our discussion of volume habits at tops and bottoms has been confined to the two general classifications of investment and speculative issues, we have, for greater accuracy, divided our index of the stocks we cover into five groups. The majority of the first two groups comprise investment stocks; groups 3 and 4, speculative stocks. The symbols, in parentheses, designate volume characteristics. The groups are as follows:

GROUP 1 (I) With but rare exceptions relative volume broadens out at bottoms and dries up at tops.

GROUP 2 (I-T) Relative volume shows a **tendency** to broaden out at bottoms and dry up at tops.

GROUP 3 (S) With but rare exceptions relative volume of stocks in this group dries up at bottoms and broadens out at tops.

GROUP 4 (S-T) Relative volume shows a **tendency** to dry up at bottoms and broaden out at tops.

GROUP 5 (X) This group has no marked volume characteristics.

According to the latest classification (August 1937), the 60 stocks which Mr. Quinn regularly studies are classified in the above categories as follows:

"The segration outlined above is based entirely upon observation of the charted volume habits of the various stocks; not upon analysis of balance sheets as a means of determining, fundamentally, whether a given stock should be classed as investment or speculative. The reason for this is that some stocks, which are of investment nature, when judged by their balance sheets alone, display speculative volume habits throughout certain phases of the business cycle. Similarly, some speculative stocks, which under certain conditions are lacking in speculative appeal, occasionally show investment volume characteristics for an extended period. Because volume habits of all stocks are not fixed, a permanent list is not published.

"As has already been mentioned, volume does not expand in **all** investment stocks as bases are being formed—nor does activity broaden in **all** speculative issues as tops are being approached. Public interest frequently ignores some stocks so that they do not perform in their customary manner. By appraising the relationship of trading from day

ACCORDING TO THE LATEST CLASSIFICATION (AUGUST 1937), THE 60 STOCKS WHICH MR. QUINN REGULARLY STUDIES ARE CLASSIFIED AS FOLLOWS:

GROUP 1 (I)	GROUP 2 (I-T)	GROUP 3 (S)	GROUP 4 (S-T)	GROUP 5 (X)
With but rare exceptions relative volume broadens out at bottoms and dries up at tops.	Relative volume shows a **tendency** to broaden out at bottoms and dry up at tops.	With but rare exceptions relative volume of stocks in this group dries up at bottoms and broadens out at tops.	Relative volume shows a **tendency** to dry up at bottoms and broaden out at tops.	This group has no marked volume characteristics.
Amer. Can	(I)	(S)	(S-T)	(X)
Amer. Telephone	(I-T)	Amer. Radiator	Allis Chalmers	Case
Corn Products	Allied Chemical	Amer. Smelting	Amer. Rolling M.	Consol. Edison
du Pont	Amer. Tobacco B	Anaconda	Briggs	Gen. Electric
Great Northern	Atchison	Balt. & Ohio	Celanese	Pennsylvania
Union Pacific	Stand. Oil of N.J.	Bendix	Chrysler	Phillips Pete.
U. S. Steel	Union Carbide	Beth. Steel	Com. Solvents	Sears Roebuck
Woolworth	Western Union	Columbia Gas	Gen. Motors	
		Dome Mines	Int. Harvester	
		Douglas	Int. Nickel	
		Elec. Auto-Lite	Johns Manville	
		Elec. Bond & Sh.	Loew's	
		Goodyear	Stand. Brands	
		Int. Telephone	Westinghouse	
		Kennecott		
		Mont. Ward		
		Nat. Distillers		
		N.Y. Central		
		North American		
		Packard		
		Pullman		
		Radio		
		Schenley		
		Sperry		
		United Aircraft		
		United Corp.		
		U.S. Smelting		

to day in groups of investments and groups of speculations, an adequate check is provided on individual stock action. Accordingly, purchase of an investment stock should normally require that it be reflecting increased relative volume as indicative of an active investment demand and that the general market as healthy. A speculative stock is not acquired until small relative volume shows that selling pressure has subsided and the market as a whole is ready to move ahead—

"Determination of selling points depends, in general, upon a similar check. If one is carrying an investment stock in which relative volume has dried up significantly, it is frequently wise to dispose of it. Lack of current interest suggests that further gains will probably be small. Likewise, speculative stocks are let go when volume broadens out to the point where a typical top formation is recognized. Whether increased activity in group 5 represents accumulation or distribution is usually determined by noting whether the Pressure Indicator is appraising the general market as strong or weak."

The author has chosen five sample Trendograph charts,* taken from Quinn's work, with the idea of generally illustrating the five categories into which Mr. Quinn divides the group of individual stocks.

In Figure 2, which shows Union Pacific, we see a stock which Quinn rates as an (I) or Investment issue, characteristically having large activity at bottoms (A) and small activity at tops (B). Although only a short period of time (March 14-October 3, 1936) is shown on this chart, a study of the previous several years shows exactly the same characteristics.

In Figure 3 we see an illustration of a Trendograph chart of American Tobacco B, which is rated as an (IT) or Investment Tendency issue. Somewhat like Union Pacific, American Tobacco B has a habit of having larger volume at bottoms (A and C) and smaller volume at tops (B), although at times this stock has fairly heavy volume at high points. Thus it cannot be given a rating as a wholly investment issue, on the basis of large volume at low points and small volume at high points.

*This refers to a chart that is no longer available.

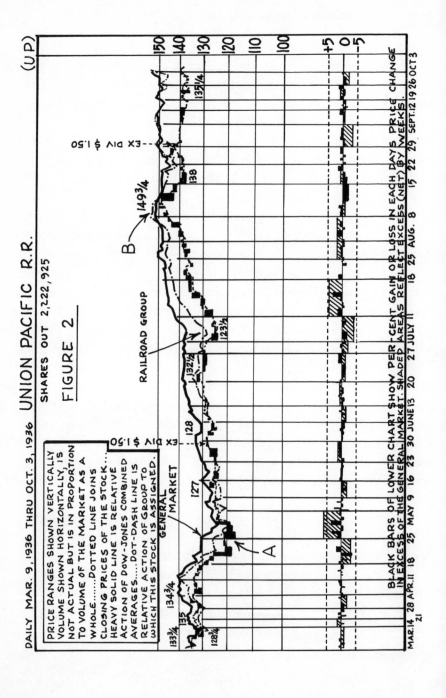

DAILY MAR. 9, 1936 THRU OCT. 3, 1936   UNION PACIFIC R.R.   (UP)

SHARES OUT 2,722,925

FIGURE 2

PRICE RANGES SHOWN VERTICALLY
VOLUME SHOWN HORIZONTALLY, IS
NOT ACTUAL BUT IS IN PROPORTION
TO VOLUME OF THE MARKET AS A
WHOLE......DOTTED LINE JOINS
CLOSING PRICES OF THE STOCK.
HEAVY SOLID LINE IS RELATIVE
ACTION OF DOW-JONES COMBINED
AVERAGES.....DOT-DASH LINE IS
RELATIVE ACTION OF GROUP TO
WHICH THIS STOCK IS ASSIGNED.

GENERAL MARKET

RAILROAD GROUP

EX DIV $ 1.50

EX DIV $ 1.50

BLACK BARS OF LOWER CHART SHOW PER-CENT GAIN OR LOSS IN EACH DAY'S PRICE CHANGE
IN EXCESS OF THE GENERAL MARKET. SHADED AREAS REFLECT EXCESS (NET) BY WEEKS.

MAR.14 28 APR.11 18 25 MAY 9 16 23 30 JUNE13 20 27 JULY11 18 25 AUG. 8 15 22 29 SEPT.12 19 26 OCT 3
     21

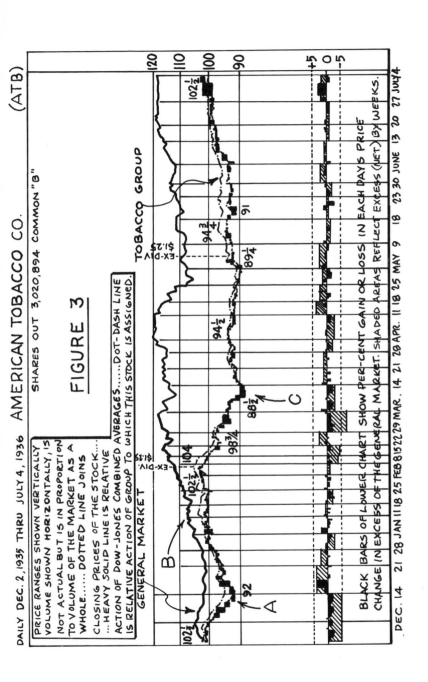

DAILY DEC. 2, 1935 THRU JULY 4, 1936   AMERICAN TOBACCO CO.   (ATB)

SHARES OUT 3,020,894 COMMON "B"

FIGURE 3

PRICE RANGES SHOWN VERTICALLY
VOLUME SHOWN HORIZONTALLY, IS
NOT ACTUAL BUT IS IN PROPORTION
TO VOLUME OF THE MARKET AS A
WHOLE......DOTTED LINE JOINS

CLOSING PRICES OF THE STOCK....
...HEAVY SOLID LINE IS RELATIVE
ACTION OF DOW-JONES COMBINED AVERAGES......DOT-DASH LINE
IS RELATIVE ACTION OF GROUP TO WHICH THIS STOCK IS ASSIGNED.

TOBACCO GROUP

GENERAL MARKET

102½   104   102½

EX-DIV. $1.25

B

A   92

98¾   88½   C

94½

89¼   94¾   91   102½

EX-DIV $1.25

120
110
100
90

+5
0
-5

BLACK BARS OF LOWER CHART SHOW PER-CENT GAIN OR LOSS IN EACH DAY'S PRICE
CHANGE (IN EXCESS OF THE GENERAL MARKET. SHADED AREAS REFLECT EXCESS (NET) BY WEEKS.

DEC. 14   21 28 JAN 11 18 25 FEB 8 15 22 29 MAR. 14 21 28 APR. 11 18 25 MAY 9   18   23 30 JUNE 13 20 27 JU'4

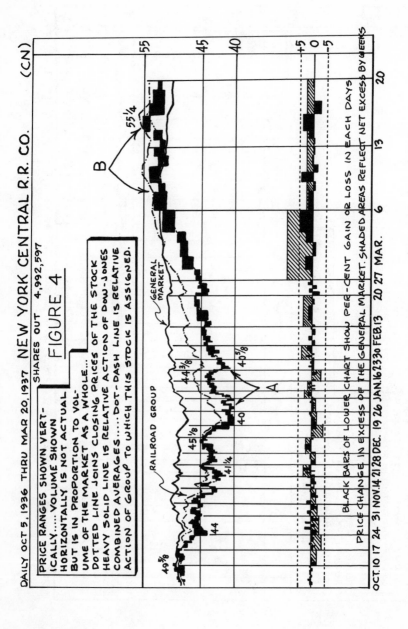

DAILY OCT 5, 1936 THRU MAR 20, 1937 NEW YORK CENTRAL R.R. CO. (CN)

SHARES OUT 4,992,597

FIGURE 4

PRICE RANGES SHOWN VERT-
ICALLY....VOLUME SHOWN
HORIZONTALLY IS NOT ACTUAL
BUT IS IN PROPORTION TO VOL-
UME OF THE MARKET AS A WHOLE...
DOTTED LINE JOINS CLOSING PRICES OF THE STOCK
HEAVY SOLID LINE IS RELATIVE ACTION OF DOW-JONES
COMBINED AVERAGES....DOT-DASH LINE IS RELATIVE
ACTION OF GROUP TO WHICH THIS STOCK IS ASSIGNED.

BLACK BARS OF LOWER CHART SHOW PER-CENT GAIN OR LOSS IN EACH DAYS
PRICE CHANGE IN EXCESS OF THE GENERAL MARKET. SHADED AREAS REFLECT NET EXCESS BY WEEKS

OCT.10 17 24· 31 NOV.14 21 28 DEC. 19 26 JAN.16 2330 FEB.13 2O 27 MAR.13 2O 27 MAR. 6 13 2O WEEKS

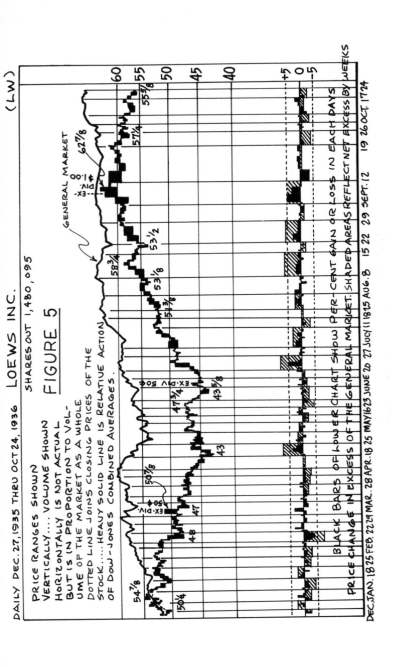

DAILY DEC. 27, 1935 THRU OCT. 24, 1936   LOEWS INC.   (LW)

SHARES OUT 1,480,095

FIGURE 5

PRICE RANGES SHOWN
VERTICALLY.... VOLUME SHOWN
HORIZONTALLY IS NOT ACTUAL
BUT IS IN PROPORTION TO VOL-
UME OF THE MARKET AS A WHOLE
DOTTED LINE JOINS CLOSING PRICES OF THE
STOCK.....HEAVY SOLID LINE IS RELATIVE ACTION
OF DOW-JONES COMBINED AVERAGES.

GENERAL MARKET

BLACK BARS OF LOWER CHART SHOW PER-CENT GAIN OR LOSS IN EACH DAYS
PRICE CHANGE IN EXCESS OF THE GENERAL MARKET. SHADED AREAS REFLECT NET EXCESS BY WEEKS

DEC. JAN. 18 25 FEB. 2229 MAR. 28 APR. 18 25 MAY 1623 JUNE 20 27 JULY 11 18 25 AUG. 8   15 22   29 SEPT. 12   19   26 OCT. 17 24

60
55
50
45
40
+5
0
-5

The chart of New York Central, which is shown on Figure 4, shows a stock rated by Quinn as a typical (S) or Speculative issue, which it truly is, with light volume at bottoms (A) and high volume at tops (B). Perhaps no better sample of a speculative issue could be used than this particular "Hope" Rail stock.

The chart of Loew's is provided as an example of the group which Mr. Quinn classifies as the (S-T) Speculative Tendency group. Lows may be expected in Loew's on light volume (no pun intended) while tops are likely to appear on large volume. But the phenomenon is not consistent although it is quite worth watching.

In Figure 6, which reflects some of the fluctuations in Consolidated Edison, we see a picture which Mr. Quinn classifies as in the (X) group, which has no marked volume characteristics. In this case it will be noted that both tops and bottoms seem to form without any notable increase in activity, as shown by the horizontal width of the rectangles showing the volume tendencies.

Continuing his interpretation, Mr. Quinn states further.

BUYING AND SELLING POINTS IN INDIVIDUAL STOCKS

"Naturally, background charts of various stocks must be studied to provide a means of studying and classifying the various issues according to their velocity characteristics in rallies and declines and their volume habits at tops and bottoms. With a knowledge of these factors, as market prices are declining, purchases are determined upon in the following manner:

"Where stocks of investment caliber are to be acquired, the charted record for various issues in this category are studied on three points.

1. Has price performance during the past year or more been satisfactory in comparison with the rest of the market?
2. From a price standpoint has the stock stood up better-than-usual in the last decline?
3. Has relative volume expanded to the point where one may reasonably conclude that this particular stock is one of those which

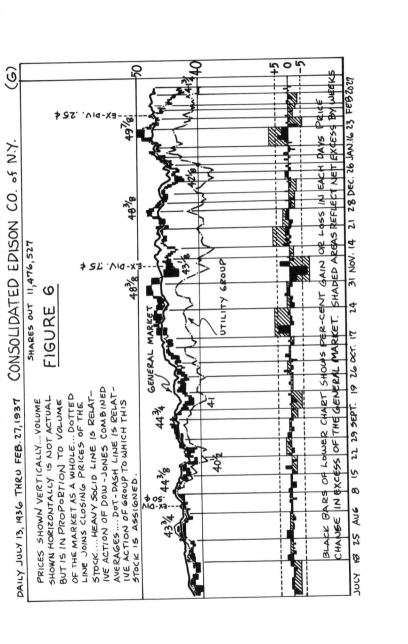

DAILY JULY 13, 1936 THRU FEB. 27, 1937   CONSOLIDATED EDISON CO. of N.Y.   (G)

SHARES OUT 11,476,527

FIGURE 6

PRICES SHOWN VERTICALLY....VOLUME
SHOWN HORIZONTALLY IS NOT ACTUAL
BUT IS IN PROPORTION TO VOLUME
OF THE MARKET AS A WHOLE... DOTTED
LINE JOINS CLOSING PRICES OF THE
STOCK.....HEAVY SOLID LINE IS RELAT-
IVE ACTION OF DOW-JONES COMBINED
AVERAGES....DOT-DASH LINE IS RELAT-
IVE ACTION OF GROUP TO WHICH THIS
STOCK IS ASSIGNED.

BLACK BARS OF LOWER CHART SHOWS PER-CENT GAIN OR LOSS IN EACH DAYS PRICE
CHANGE IN EXCESS OF THE GENERAL MARKET. SHADED AREAS REFLECT NET EXCESS BY WEEKS

JULY 18 25 AUG 8 15 22 29 SEPT. 19 26 OCT. 17 24 31 NOV. 14 21 28 DEC. 26 JAN. 16 23 FEB 20 27 is being singled out as representing better-than-average value?

If the answer to these three questions is in the affirmative, purchases may be made with reasonable assurance.

"A similar procedure is followed in determining upon the purchase of speculative stocks except with respect to point No. 3. Speculative stocks normally make bottoms to the accompaniment of small relative volume, as a consequence, we look for a significant narrowing down in our rectangles as evidence of lack of selling pressure. It is important, too, in studying the record for approximately the past year to determine whether or not it embraces a period of major distribution at a level above that at which the stock is currently priced. Where a condition of this kind exists, an approach to the past distribution area in all probability encounters so much supply as seriously to impair the forward move (lower tops). Points of major distribution are recognized by extreme width in the daily rectangles.

"When the general price trend turns upward after a base has been formed, speculative stocks are purchased as so-called 'buying signals' are seen. These develop under increased activity and favorable price action and usually are found within a single day's performance.

"If, after a decrease in relative volume in a decline, activity broadens out on a single day to the accompaniment of a percentage increase in price greater than that seen in the market as a whole, we can conclude (a) that there is a trend on interest toward this stock, and (b) that this increased interest is favorable. Usually, but not always, relative volume in a dependable buying signal will be greater than in any of the five preceding days.

"The three following rules appear to embrace most of the fundamentals necessary for profitable operation:

"Rule No. 1—A buying point is usually indicated when relative volume shows an appreciable increase accompanied by a reasonably proportionate increase in the price of the stock in excess of the average.

"Rule No. 2—A stop-loss order should be placed below the closing price of the stock on the first day following that in which it shows a price loss on the average of any extent at all, accompanied by relative volume equal to 50% or more of that which has gone immediately before.

"Rule No. 3—A stop-loss order should be placed below the closing price of a stock on the first day following that in which the stock gained little on the average despite unusually large relative volume.

"Observation suggests that stops should be placed about 10% below closing prices for low-priced stocks and about 5% for high-priced stocks. 'Open' stop orders should always be used. Placing stops too close behind an active issue is likely to take you out on the bottom of a small recession.

"The comparative price gain one should look for depends upon the stock's velocity characteristics. If it is a fast mover, a comparatively large gain in excess of the market—say, 5% or more—should be seen. Just what this percentage should be can best be determined by checking the past record and noting those patterns which later on proved to have been dependable.

"Those who are carrying investment stocks watch relative volume as prices advance. In a major move, it will frequently be found that one issue, upon reaching certain levels, will lose its following, as evidenced by a continued decrease in relative activity. If the market is still strong, funds in such issues can often be switched advantageously to other situations which have been late in getting started, but currently are showing a more active investment demand. When, however, the point is reached where the market is given over largely to speculation all investment stocks should either be sold or profits protected with stop-loss orders.

"In speculative stocks we know that tops normally are seen to the accompaniment of a broadening out in relative volume. Just so long as this widening out in the charted rectangles is supported by **propor-**

tionate comparative price gains, it may be assumed that the supply-demand situation is satisfactory. As the time approaches when, perhaps under still greater activity, comparative price gains are insignificant or lacking, then it is obvious that the supply-demand relationship has deteriorated and profit taking is impeding a continuation of the advance.

"Under these conditions, if the market as a whole appears to be reasonably healthy, it is usually desirable to protect profits with stops or to switch funds to other speculative situations in which supply has not yet been encountered."

There is no question about the fact that Quinn's studies of price-volume relations represent research of considerable importance.

He has developed an index which he calls a "Pressure Indicator", for the purpose of measuring the relation of supply and demand, with the object of determining the technical position of the market as a whole. This was first published in 1933, and during 1934 and 1935 it had a fairly good record of accuracy in forecasting the important intermediate turning points. But at the April 1936 and the March 1937 highs the index failed to forecast growing weakness prior to substantial declines. And so in May of 1937 Quinn revised his "Pressure Indicator" and published an entirely new index, which as yet has not been tested by a period of actual market practice. This revised "Pressure Indicator" appears to present a considerable problem in interpretation, and for that reason this author chooses to withhold judgment on its value.

The general approach of the Trendograph chart, as illustrated in Figures 2-6, must be credited as a sound one, but unless the trader subscribes to the service and receives each week the 60 individual charts, the labor involved in making a chart of this kind for any substantial number of stocks is extensive, and unless the trader has a substantial interest in a few particular issues the effort involved is great. Nevertheless, the method evolved by Quinn of studying the price-volume relation may certainly be credited as one of the greatest advances in the field.

OTHER VOLUME STUDIES

Before proceeding to a brief summary of the subject of Volume let us consider it from several other angles. Earlier in the Chapter, it was noticed that some market students attempt to study what might be called price-volume velocity by relating price changes and volume mathematically.

The usual method, it was noted, is to divide volume by price change, with the idea of finding out what amount of volume is required for a given gain or loss in price.

The theory of these studies is that when an advance meets a preponderance of supply volume the upward changes, or advances, will be accompanied by an increased amount of turnover as compared with the amount of advance; and declines will be accompanied by an increased turnover. Conversely, the theory is that during a price decline, when an increase in activity does not result in a proportionate decline in price, a bottom is not far away.

Let us examine Figure 7, as an illustration of the principle. Unfortunately, as noted previously, these studies do not show uniform phenomena.

Figure 7, shows the hourly price movements from September 4 to September 21, 1935, inclusive. The upper series of black bars drawn downward toward the price trend represent those hours which were declines; while the lower series of bars drawn upward to the price trend designate those hours in which there were price advances. Both series of black bars show the relative amount of volume as compared with the price change, which is obtained by dividing the hourly volume in each successive case by the net change in price, and plotting the resulting quotients in the top series, if they represent minuses or declines, and in the bottom series if they represent pluses or advances.

Although this particular illustration shows the hourly index, the same principle may be applied to daily or weekly charts. The formula consists of two simple steps in arithmetic: (1) find the price change, desig-

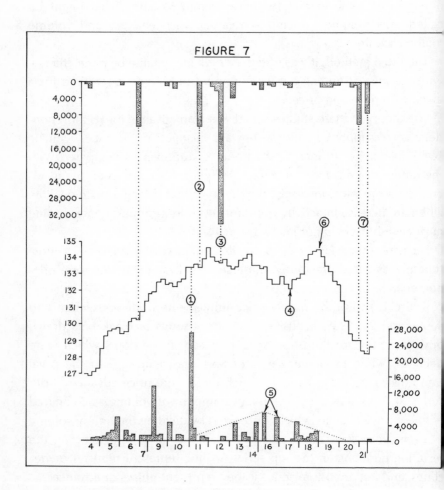

FIGURE 7

nating it minus or plus, and (2) divide it into the volume for the time period (hourly, daily, weekly), and plot the figure so obtained on a center line graph, from figures below it. The arrangement in Figure 7 is a convenient one.

Now let us look at Figure 7. Here we see an advance from the first hour September 4 to the last hour September 11, a decline from that point to the third hour September 17. This was followed by a short advance to the last hour September 18, and finally there was a decline to the first hour September 21.

The questions which arise are: Did this statistical study show evidence of the top at the last hour on September 11; the bottom in the third hour September 17; the top in the last hour September 18; and the low point in the last hour September 21.

The phenomena we see in Figure 7 are typical of such studies. Dotted lines have been projected from the bars showing significant volume-price changes to the price line. It is interesting to note that as the advance from September 4 reached the high on September 11, substantial volume on the upside at (1) failed to result in a proportionate increase in price to that in previous hours.

Also, as this top was reached, there were two occasions when there were substantial increases in volume (2 and 3), when price declines occurred just before and at the top. Together, these signalled a turn.

So far, so good—the theory outlined above appears correct. But let us take the low which terminated the decline from September 11 to September 17. Theoretically, we might have seen here, in the middle hour of September 17, at (4), some increase in volume, as shown by black bars at the top, without comparable price recession. Instead, all that the chart showed was a moderate increase of activity during two price advances (5), several hours before the bottom.

Next, according to the theory, we should have seen some increase in volume, as shown in the lower series, as the top of September 18 was reached (6) indicating that activity was increasing without price advance, or conversely that during minor declines, volume was increasing, as might have been seen in the upper series. Actually, there was no important indication.

The bottom on September 21 was signalled somewhat better, in that after a steady decline, in the last hour September 18, when the majority of price changes were downward, there was a substantial increase in volume proportionate to price change, in the fourth hour September 20 and the first hour September 21, (7) which helped to signal the upside reversal.

The shortcoming of this type of study is that sometimes it produces valuable indications, of a reversal point, and at other times a turning point goes without any indications whatsoever.

VOLUME AND FIGURE CHARTS

With the exception of some minor trend charts, wherein the volume is accumulated and plotted for every fluctuation of $1/8$ in an individual stock, volume is seldom studied in connection with figure charts, except where the figure chartist refers to a bar chart of the market as a whole.

Many figure chart students contend that volume is an unreliable indicator, and that the price trend shows all that they need. But perhaps the chief reason why figure chart students do not employ a study of volume is because it is almost impossible to plot it on a figure chart.

"NEVER SELL A DULL MARKET SHORT"

This is an old Wall Street axiom, which we hear more often in bear markets than in bull markets. It is **not,** by any means, always true. Let us take Figures 8 and 9 to illustrate our point. In the case shown in Figure 8, volume goes dull, or dries up on a reaction in an uptrend, and

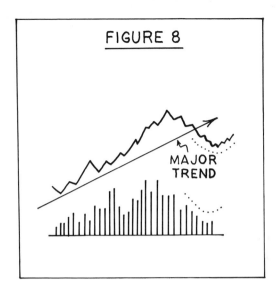

FIGURE 8

MAJOR TREND

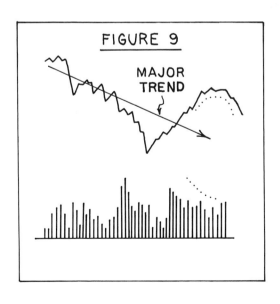

FIGURE 9

MAJOR TREND

the axiom holds true only too well. But in the case of Figure 9, volume goes dull after a correction on the upside has spent itself, just before downtrend is resumed. The latter case is typical of not only the minor trends in bear markets, but also the corrective phases of bear market intermediate cycles. Upon several occasions in the 1929-1932 bear market, the first minor reaction from the intermediate tops was accompanied by a decrease in activity just as some of the best selling opportunities developed.

It might be good practice never to sell a dull market short in a corrective decline of an upward trend, but many opportunities would be lost by not selling a dull market short after a corrective rally in a bear market. The importance of the axiom appears to depend upon the direction of the major trend.

Thus, we may profitably amend the axiom, and say: "Never sell a dull market short in a major upward trend." Let us take as two examples periods during 1932. In the last week of March, just before the three-months' trading area was broken, and the drastic decline which ended with the July bottoms of 1932 developed, the market was exceedingly dull, and the trader had every reason to believe that the floor of the trading area had been reached. That dullness might easily have been interpreted as a bullish signal, indicating that a rise from the floor of this trading area might ensue. Instead, a terrific decline developed.

Let us look at another case in the first ten days of July, 1932 when the bear market ended. Here is a case where, unlike March, the dullness was one of the most important signals of a coming advance which turned out to be a major reversal.

If we lay down the new axiom as a general rule which has exceptions, we might also say, conversely: "Never buy a dull bear market".[*]

---

[*]Fred S. McClafferty, in his "A Course in Trading," published by the Wetsel Market Bureau, suggested these variations of the original axiom, which appear to be very sound.

SUMMARY

Although many pages have been spent in discussing the subject of Volume, and it has been reviewed from many different angles, we can reduce its practical use for the average reader to a few simple ideas, which we may summarize as follows:

1. Avoid inactive stocks, unless you are interested chiefly in the long term trend, because their thin markets make it almost impossible to conduct advantageous trading. (S.E.C. regulation has emphasized this axiom.)
2. If you are interested in the minor trend, by all means confine your trading to the leading issues which are included in the 50 most active stocks, over a period of the preceding year.
3. Never neglect the consideration of volume. If an active stock becomes inactive, do not continue to trade in it.
4. Stocks of companies with small capitalizations are not necessarily the best trading mediums. They are often very volatile issues which have thin markets and move rapidly. Successful trading in such issues depends on keeping one's eyes glued to the tape. Large capitalizations are not necessarily a drawback to the trader. General Motors and U. S. Steel are good examples of this contention.
5. Remember that the relative changes in volume are far more important than the actual changes, because all during an active period the trading in almost every stock expands.
6. When a volume ratio, which represents true relative volume, rises to a sharp peak as compared with its performance for a year or eighteen months previously, if an advance or decline of two or three weeks has been under way, look for a turning point. On the other hand, if the price trend of a leading stock has been moving sidewise, and suddenly resumes a diagonal direction, if the volume ratio rises sharply it is usually a good signal that a new diagonal trend of importance is under way. If

the move is up, buy the stock on the next reaction. If the move is down, sell the stock on the next rally.

7. Remember that various stocks have different characteristics at reversal points. As a general proposition, a speculative issue will show increased activity during a rise, and a peak of volume preceding or near a top. Conversely, it will show a decrease in activity during a price decline, and a low level of trading near a bottom (in a bull market).

   As a general proposition, investment stocks will show a tendency for activity to increase in a decline, and reach a peak near a bottom, while conversely, activity in investment stocks tends to decrease in price advances, and be at a relatively low level compared with the general market volume, when tops are reached. However, these characteristics are not permanent or unchanging, thus the volume characteristics of various stocks must be scrutinized constantly to see possible changes.

8. After a long decline has taken place and the price trend begins to rise, an increase of volume on minor rallies and a decrease on minor declines is of important bullish significance. Conversely, after an extended advance, a decrease of volume on minor rallies and an increase on minor declines is of important bearish significance.

9. As a general rule, volume decreases during a bear market and increases during a bull market. The peaks of volume in bull markets appear **just preceding** the intermediate tops, near the end of major phases. The highest points of volume are seldom at exactly the top levels.

10. During a corrective phase of a bull market, one of the characteristics in judging its termination is a steady decrease in volume, with activity at a low level as the correction reaches its termination, just before the resumption of the major uptrend.

11. In bear markets, selling climaxes are accompanied by a sharp increase in volume, as panic reaches its peak. During rallies in

bear markets (corrective phases), volume shows a tendency to decrease from the high level of the selling climax, but will frequently rise at the top of the corrective phase.

12. Whenever a trend line or moving average, or the upper or lower limit of a Dow Theory "line", or a previous high or low is penetrated, an increase in volume is considered a confirming factor. If the breakaway from the apex of a triangle is accompanied by an increase in activity, it is less likely to be a false one than a movement which occurs on dullness.

Part V

Contemporary Wisdom

It was a long, hard climb, but in the prosperous years following World War II the market finally began to stir the imagination of the public again. It took the Industrials 25 years—until 1954—to recover their 1929 levels. The Rails and Utilities were even slower; it took them 35 years—until 1964—to come back to 1929 levels. In many ways, Wall Street of the Fifties and Sixties started out as a safer and saner place than it had been in the frenzied Twenties. While it still retained many of its old habits and customs, it learned some new tricks. Thus, the contemporary market sages, speaking from their present vantage point, command the special attention of a new generation of investors attempting the age-old profit-making strategies.

BENJAMIN GRAHAM . . The Father of Fundamental Analysis.

HUMPHREY NEILL . . Wall Street Contrarian.

GERALD M. LOEB . . "The Wizard of Wall Street".

GARFIELD A. DREW . . Columbus of the Odd-Lot Theory.

ROBERT D. EDWARDS and JOHN MAGEE . . Master Chart Interpreters.

DR. LEO BARNES . . Collector of Profitable Stock Market Ideas.

BENJAMIN GRAHAM

The Father of Fundamental Security Analysis

It may seem strange to newcomers that anyone still living could merit the label "Father of Security Analysis" when individual stocks have been studied for some 175 years in this country. Yet it is true, for Benjamin Graham is generally credited with the first really penetrating brand of almost scientific security analysis. His concepts are source material for today's fundamental analysis.

As were a surprising number of "greats" in the investment world, Benjamin Graham was born in London, on May 9, 1894. But unlike the others, he was brought to the USA as an infant, in 1895 (and naturalized in 1921).

After gaining a BS degree at Columbia in 1914, at the age of 20, he began working for Newburger, Henderson and Loeb, where he remained until 1923. From 1921-1923 he was a junior partner in the firm (achieving this rank at the age of 27), where he managed investment portfolios.

In 1945, he became president of the Graham-Newman Corporation. Among other posts he has held: director, Government Employees Insurance Co., governor, New York Institute of Finance (where he lectured on security analysis), and more recently, Regents Professor of Finance, University of California at Los Angeles.

But it is in his written works that Graham has made his real mark on Wall Street. His *Security Analysis,* now in its fourth edition, (McGraw-Hill), is the definitive work in its field. In both this book and his more popular *Intelligent Investor,* Graham takes a pro-investment line to stock purchase. He frowns on stock speculation, feeling that there are no sound principles to guide the speculator in the market.

The Wisdom of
BENJAMIN GRAHAM

Stock Selection

THE SELECTION OF common stocks for the portfolio of the defensive investor is a relatively simple matter. Here we would suggest four rules to be followed:

(1) There should be adequate though not excessive diversification. This might mean a minimum of ten different issues and a maximum of about thirty.

(2) Each company selected should be large, prominent, and conservatively financed. Indefinite as these adjectives must be, their general sense is clear.

(3) Each company should have a long record of continuous dividend payments. The acid test is the payment of dividends during the great depression years, 1931-33. We are reluctant, however, to include 1931-33 dividend payments as a positive requirement here. It would mean carrying the test of investment quality too far backward into the past and thus into circumstances that may no longer be sufficiently relevant to future probabilities. As a logical compromise we would suggest the requirement of continuous dividend payments beginning at least in 1936. This would cover the period now generally referred to as "pre-war."

(4) The price paid for each should be reasonable in relation to its average earnings for the last five years or longer. We would recommend a price not to exceed twenty times such earnings. (Until a record of post-war earnings has been established, we suggest also a price not to exceed twenty-five times the 1936-40 earnings.) This would protect the investor against the common error of buying good stocks at high levels of the general market. It would also bar the purchase, even in normal markets, of a number of fine issues which sell at unduly high prices in anticipation of greatly increased future earnings. We feel that such common stocks are not appropriate for the defensive investor who should not be called upon to use the judgment and foresight necessary to avoid errors in this field.

Investment Company Shares

THE INVESTOR WITH a common stock fund of under $15,000 would be well advised to acquire his list indirectly, through the medium of investment company shares. Most of the shares now being purchased are issued by so-called "open end" companies, which sell their securities continuously through distributing organizations. The price charged includes a mark-up for selling costs, which tend to run about eight per cent of the value of the underlying assets. The shares may be sold back to the company at any time at the then asset value.

Rules for the Appraisal of Common Stocks

(1) The appraised value is determined by (a) estimating the earning power, (b) applying thereto a suitable multiplier, and (c) adjusting, if necessary, for asset value.

(2) The earning power should ordinarily represent an estimate of average earnings for the next five years.

(3) The above estimate should be developed preferably from a projection of the dollar volume and the profit margin. The starting point is the actual exhibit over some period in the past. Under conditions existing in early 1949 there is no "normal period" of past years which can be accepted as a direct measure of future earning power. However, an averaging of the results of an unusually good period and a subnormal period might be acceptable, i.e., giving 50 per cent weight to the 1936-40 average after taxes and 50 per cent weight to 1947-48 or 1946-48.

(4) When figures of earlier years enter into the calculation, proper adjustment should be made for subsequent changes in capitalization.

(5) The multiplier should reflect prospective longer term changes in earnings. A multiplier of 12 is suitable for stocks with neutral prospects. Increases or decreases from this figure must depend on the judgment and preferences

of the appraiser. In all but the most exceptional cases, however, the maximum multiplier should be 20 and the minimum should be 8.

(6) If the tangible-asset value is less than the earning-power value (earning power times multiplier), the latter may be reduced by some arbitrary factor to reflect this deficiency. Our suggested factor is as follows: Deduct one-quarter of the amount by which the earning-power value exceeds twice the asset value. (This permits a 100 per cent premium over tangible assets without penalty.)

(7) If the net-current-asset value exceeds the earning-power value, the latter may be increased by 50 per cent of the excess to give the final appraised value.

(8) Where extraordinary conditions prevail—such as war profits or war restrictions, or a temporary royalty or rental situation—the amount of the total probable gain or loss per share due to such conditions should be estimated and added to, or subtracted from, the appraised value as determined without considering the abnormal conditions.

(9) Where the capitalization structure is highly speculative—that is, where the total of senior securities is disproportionately large—then the value of the entire enterprise should first be determined as if it had common stock only. This value should be apportioned between the senior securities and the common stock on a basis which recognizes the going-concern value of the senior claims. (Note difference between this treatment and a valuation based on dissolution rights of the senior securities.) If an adjustment is needed for extraordinary conditions, as referred to in (8), this should be made in the total enterprise value, not on a per-share-of common basis.

(10) The more speculative the position of the common stock—for whatever reason—the less practical dependence can be accorded to the appraised value found.

(11) Appraised values should be taken as a definite guide to current purchase or sale only if they exceed or fall below the market price by at least one-third. In other cases they may be useful as a supplemental fact in analysis and investment decisions.

Investment in Giant Enterprises

N 1947 *Business Week* ran a little article on the "Billion Dollar Club," in which it referred to American businesses with either assets or sales exceeding $1 billion. In addition to thirty-one banks and insurance companies there were six railroads, three utilities, and nine industrials in this category, as follows:

Railroads: Atchison, B. & O., N. Y. Central, Pennsylvania, Southern Pacific, and Union Pacific.

Utilities: American Tel. & Tel., Commonwealth & Southern, and Consolidated Edison of N.Y.

Industrials: Armour, Great Atlantic & Pacific, Du Pont, General Motors, Sears Roebuck, Standard Oil of N.J., Swift, U.S. Steel.

All of these enterprises have achieved enormous size, and by that token they have presumably made a great success. But how successful are they from the standpoint of the investor? We must first supply our definition of success in this context:

"A successful listed company is one which earns sufficient to justify an average valuation of its shares in excess of the invested capital behind them."

This means that to be really successful (or prosperous) the company must have an earning power value which exceeds the amount invested by and for the stockholder. In the aggregate the industrial issues listed on the New York Stock Exchange sold for more than book value in 1947, and this was true for about three-quarters of the companies in the Dow-Jones Industrial List. The companies in the "billion-dollar club," however, do not show up so well. Only four of the industrials, one of the utilities, and none of the rails sold on the average in 1947 as high as book value. Similarly, most of these issues sold at lower prices in 1947 than they did in 1927. Far from showing the dynamic qualities of growth issues, the group as a whole was unable to maintain its market position vis-a-vis common stocks generally.

If similar data were compiled for the nineteen banking institutions in the billion-dollar class, we are sure they would fail to meet our tests of prosperous operation from the stockholder's standpoint.

It is evident from this analysis that the biggest companies are not the best companies to invest in. (Federal Trade Commission data on the percentage earned on invested capital support this conclusion.) It is equally true that small-sized companies are not suited to the needs of the average investor, although there may be remarkable opportunities in individual concerns in this field. There is some basis here for suggesting that defensive investors show preference to companies in the asset range between $50 million and $250 million, although we have no idea of propounding this as a hard-and-fast rule.

HUMPHREY
NEILL

Wall Street Contrarian

Thinking along "unfashionable" lines has always had a certain following. But the leading exponent of Contrary Opinion with regard to the market in the postwar world has been Humphrey Neill.

If the nation thinks peace, he is likely to think war; if the nation thinks war he may think peace. It is not just "opposite" thinking, but rather a refined process and a re-refining to see if what is expected to happen is truly LIKELY to happen. It's an art.

Humphrey Bancroft Neill was born January 21, 1895 in Buffalo, New York. His first writing efforts were in the field of advertising. He has been an economic journalist and business writer most of his life. He lays no claim to being a professional economist; rather prefers to consider himself a socio-economic journalist.

Sometime after he had established the theory on contrary thinking in a formal fashion in 1940, he began publishing, at irregular intervals, an opinion letter. In 1949 it became a fortnightly affair called the Fraser-Neill Letter (together with James L. Fraser).

The service proclaims to discuss business, finance and socio-economics, but in fact it also covers any and all pertinent matters and dwells frequently on the stock market. Politics is a regular subject visitor also. The service is published in Wells, Vermont.

325

The Wisdom of
HUMPHREY NEILL

Thoughts on the Contrary Opinion Approac

BECAUSE A CROWD does not think but acts on
impulses, public opinions are frequently wrong.
By the same token because a crowd is carried away
by feeling, or sentiment, you will find the public participating enthusiastically in various manias **after** the mania
has got well under momentum. This is illustrated in the
stock market. The crowd—the public—will remain in-
different when prices are low and fluctuating but little.
The public is attracted by activity and by the movement
of prices. It is especially attracted by **rising** prices. Thus,
in former days a "crowd" could be tempted into the
market when a manipulator made a stock active and
pushed its price higher.

Is the public wrong **all the time?**

The answer is, decidedly, "No." The public is perhaps
right more of the time than not. In stock-market parlance,
the public is right **during** the trends but wrong at both
ends!

One can assert that the public is usually wrong at
junctures of events and at terminals of trends.

So, to be cynical, you might say, "Yes, the public is always wrong when **it pays to be right**—but is far from wrong in the meantime.

It is to be noted that the use of contrary opinions will frequently result in one's being rather **too** far ahead of events. A contrary opinion will seldom "time" one's conclusions accurately.

If one relies on the Theory of Contrary Opinion for accurate timing of his decisions he frequently will be disappointed.

Having concentrated for many years on the study of the Theory of Contrary Opinion (and having put my thoughts on paper), I believe it is correct to say that the theory is more valuable in **avoiding** errors in forecasting than in employing it for definite forecasting.

*   *   *   *   *   *

Let us quickly define that harsh word "gregarious." It means "associating together in herds"—from the Latin word for "Flock."

One of the books found helpful in a study of the art of contrary thinking is *Instincts of the Herd in Peace and War*,* by William Trotter. The author bases his sociological thesis on "gregarious man," or the herd instincts in us humans. He asserts that "man is a gregarious animal in literal fact, that he is as essentially gregarious as the bee and the ant, the sheep, the ox, and the horse . . . and that his (man's) conduct furnished incontestable proof of this thesis, which is thus an indispensable clue to any inquiry into the intricate problems of human society.

Very briefly, with the risk of lifting thoughts out of context let us extract Trotter's summary of the more obvious gregarious characteristics we display:

(1) Man is intolerant and fearful of solitude—physical or mental. (I think we all recognize this general characteristic. The vast majority of people dislike to be alone. If we have to spend a day all by ourselves, most of us become bored with our own company within the first hour.)

(2) He is more sensitive to the voice of the herd than to any other

---

*Published by Ernest Benn, Ltd., London.

influence. (This, of course, is the theory of "Following the crowd.")

(3) He is subject to passions of the pack in his mob violence and the passions of the herd in panics. (Economic panics reflect this characteristic also.)

(4) He is remarkably susceptible to leadership. (One immediately thinks of Hitler or Napoleon, but history books contain countless stories of mob leadership.)

(5) His relations with his fellows are dependent upon the recognition of him as a member of the herd. (Here we get into the psychological excuses for "popularity contests," and into the field of modern personnel work and into the new science of "human relations in industry.")

If the habit of contrary thinking does no more than to teach us to develop our own resources—**and to like to be alone occasionally**—it would be worth while; because when alone we might fall into the habit of actually thinking through a given subject, instead of taking the other fellow's word for it. (As one writer has said: If you cannot think through a subject you're through thinking.) If we can learn to think we shall indeed be a member of the **minority!** An aid to thinking is found by taking prominent assertions and allowing your mind to roam over all the "opposites" and "alternates" you can think of. I call this ruminating (or chewing the cud).

This question bobs up constantly: What **is** this theory of contrary opinion?

The reply may be stated in a word: It is a "way" of thinking, but, let me add, let's not overweigh it! Let us give it its proper weight.

Law of Universal Inequality

WHEN THE SOCIAL falsifiers, with their pernicious propaganda, try to make us believe that there should be full equality among everybody, let us contrary realists take heed of Pareto's Law of Universal **In**-equality.

Vilfredo Pareto (1848-1923) was a brilliant engineer, born in Paris of Italian parentage. His discovery of the "distribution of incomes" became known as Pareto's Law while the graphic representation of his law is known as the Pareto Curve.

According to Carl Snyder, Pareto's Law states, in simplest terms, "that the larger incomes are received by comparatively few people, the number with low incomes are more numerous, and as the incomes decrease the number receiving these lower incomes steadily increases in a very smooth curve.

"If we represent graphically by logarithms the various levels of income and the number of persons in receipt of each level of income, the 'curve' so drawn will be a straight line (with minor discrepancies at the extremes of the curve)."

Of what good is Pareto's Law you may be asking yourself. Everyone knows there are millions more poor people than rich ones.

The basic concept that is so important in this law is that those nations which have developed the largest wealthy classes also have the highest standard of living among **all** the population. A moment's reflection on the comparison between, say China and the United States will emphasize this.

Moreover, any long-run **lowering** of the incomes of the top groups will **decrease** the incomes of those all the way down to the bottom. Perhaps it would be clearer to say that any shrinkage in the large income groups would cause a lowering of the standard of living of the groups below. (Short run income decreases, due to temporary heavy taxation, are not considered.)

So, when the social experimenters talk to you about equalizing incomes you can turn to Pareto's Law and demonstrate that if incomes are equalized they will be equalized at **low** levels—and, further, that as time passes the standard of living will sink to the levels of those nations which have relatively few rich.

General welfare is derived from **more** crumbs falling off the **increasing numbers** of wealthy tables; not by taking away the tables and making everybody eat at a trough.

Is the Public Always Wrong
in the Market?

THIS QUESTION COMES up repeatedly during any discussion of the contrary theory. It is natural that it should come up, because the idea of money-making the easy way is a popular pastime. And of course it's a fallacy!

Perhaps no undertaking is more difficult than playing the stock market. Only a tiny fraction of those who attempt this "easy way to riches" ever succeed. What defeats them is a little matter of inherent characteristics. (1) A few persons are endowed with the money-making attribute (this, to my mind, you're born with; and if you haven't got it, you'd better forget it! I believe people either have a "money mind" or they haven't); (2) Additionally various human traits stand in the way of this pleasant method of getting rich without working for it, such as the emotional drawbacks of fear, hope, greed, wishful-thinking, and so on.

From these references you can see why the public is wrong so frequently in the stock market. However, a fairly correct, generalized reply to the question in the heading above might be expressed this way:

The "Crowd" has always been found to be wrong when it counted most to be right. This is a bit quippish; a more sedate reply would be that the crowd is wrong at the **terminals** of trends, but it is right, on the average, **during** the trends.

You find the public aiding and "pushing" the trends (up and down), —more actively when the stock market is going up than when it is in a prolonged bear trend. The public loses heart quickly when prices continue to slide off. Thus, we find public selling often increasing as the slide deepens; until finally, near the bottom "when all hope is lost" people dump their stocks—at a time when they should be picking up the bargains.

One might suppose from this that a simple formula of acting in a contrary manner would make it easy to rake in the profits.

However, those traits of human nature have to be dealt with, and they are obstinate obstructionists indeed! Above all, what makes it practically impossible to beat the game is the trait of IMPATIENCE.

Advice on Trading

THIS COUNSEL MAY be the most important I can suggest: trade alone. Close your mind to the opinions of others; pay no attention to outside influences. Disregard reports, rumors, and idle board-room chatter. If you are going to trade actively, and are going to employ your own judgment, then for heaven's sake, stand or fall by your own opinions.

If we all would trade only when the trend is definitely indicated and then patiently wait until the action signifies the probable termination of the move, how much larger our profits would be! Six to twelve successful trades a year, based upon the important, intermediate trends will return far greater profits than countless attempts within the minor fluctuations, whereby a large number of losses must ensue and where profits will be small.

GERALD M. LOEB

The Wizard of Wall Street

Gerald M. Loeb wrote a book that probably has had more printings since its first edition in 1937 than any book in the history of U. S. financial literature. In that book, as in all his pronouncements he puts forth his basic philosophy that **"FINANCIAL SAFETY LIES ONLY IN DOING THE RIGHT THING WITH MONEY . . . FORGET DIVIDENDS . . . LOOK TO CAPITAL GAINS."**

Loeb was born in 1899 in San Francisco, where he was educated. At 21 he began as a bond salesman for a retail bond dealer in San Francisco. The job lasted only three days because Loeb couldn't sell a share of a security he didn't believe in. His next job was with a NYSE firm in San Francisco, directing people to a customers' man. But many mistook him for a salesman so he took orders and built up 85 customers in 9 months. He put in a 14-hour day, working and studying.

From the start Loeb was his own best customer. One of his principles: "You can't sell anything to anybody if you can't sell it first to yourself." Though employed in the bond department, his interest was heavily in stocks. He wrote signed articles for the San Francisco *Call* and *Post* and other newspapers starting in 1921; they achieved a wide following.

After nine months he left this job (for somewhat similar

reasons to his first quitting), and became San Francisco manager of the Statistical Department of E. F. Hutton and Co. (at the age of 22) taking his 85 customers with him. But before starting the job he went to New York—though he couldn't afford it—to see Wall Street and make contacts. This furthered his career immeasurably. He came back from New York to the west coast brimming with information that would prove to be of great value to his clients.

In 1924 young Loeb returned to New York to stay. Eventually, he rose to partnership in E. F. Hutton and Co., in the course of which he became a millionaire, trading for his own and his customers' accounts. He is constantly asked, by a varied range of publications, for his opinion on the health of the market. If Wall Street has any royalty, G. M. Loeb is one of the leading blue bloods; if not indeed a pretender to the throne.

Loeb's foremost book is *The Battle for Investment Survival*, which has been referred to for so long that people just call it *The Battle*. In 1960 he authored a very slim but useful volume entitled *Loeb's Checklist for Buying Stocks*. Both are published by Simon & Schuster, Publishers.

The Wisdom of
GERALD M. LOEB

Trends and Psychology

(FROM "THE BATTLE FOR INVESTMENT SURVIVAL," 1935)

THERE IS ROOM for much improvement in the average run of statistical analysis attempting to appraise the value of a particular issue. Most of the time the figures considered are not, in my opinion, the useful and vital ones at all, and generally the whole method of approach is academic and theoretical, neglecting fundamental trends which are far more important than statistics on individual issues.

In my opinion, the primary factor in securing market profits lies in sensing the general trend. Are we in a deflation or inflation period? If the former, I would hardly bother to analyze most equities. I have known people to go to the expense of securing a thorough field report on a company, complete except for proper consideration of market factors, buying the stock because of the report and later losing a fortune in it at a time when a market study would have suggested that all equities should be avoided. And I have seen individuals make a great deal of money buying, without much study of individual issues, the leading stocks under circumstances that suggested a fall in money and a rise in shares. Thus effort should be concentrated first on deciding the trend and next in seeking out the most responsive stocks.

I certainly feel that it is more feasible to try to follow profitably a trend upwards or downwards than to attempt to determine the price level. I do not think anyone really knows when a particular security is "cheap" or "dear" in the sense that cheapness would occur around a real market bottom and dearness around a real top. For example, shares have a habit of sometimes seeming dear in the early stages of an advance, and later at far higher levels new and unexpected developments often make them seem cheap again. There is no rule about it.

I have seen stocks make bottoms when they seemed so cheap that one actually mistrusted one's intelligence, and I have seen bottoms reached at times that suggested to the majority that the shares in question were actually a good short sale. The reverse is true for bull-market tops. The money that has been lost "feeling" for the bottom or top never has been generally appreciated. The totals, if they could be known, must be staggering. Naturally we are concerned only with factors influencing security prices that are open to successful interpretation. It would be satisfying always to buy on the bottom and sell on the top, but as we do not know how to determine the bottoms and tops and would lose too much trying to guess, then of course it is only logical to turn our attention to those profitable methods we might actually learn to follow.

The most important single factor in shaping security markets is public psychology. This is really another reason why I am not particularly impressed with academic calculations purporting to show what this or that stock should be worth unless due regard is given to market factors. I feel that the psychology which leads people to pay forty times net (to use that yardstick for an example) for a stock under one set of conditions and refuse to buy the same shares under another set of conditions at ten times is such a powerful and vital price-changing factor that it can overshadow actual earnings trends as an influence on stock prices.

On Tape Reading

I N MY OPINION, far and away the most important thing to master in Wall Street is the tape. It is possible to see only the tape, and nothing else, and make a lot of money. It is a safety valve and automatic check on everything you do if you understand how to read it.

My strong belief in this point of view is another compelling reason for my early insistence on active listed leaders. The best means for judging the rest is simply not at hand. Dealing in outside stocks or bonds without benefit of an active quoted auction market is like firing a steam boiler without a safety valve, or running a train with the signal system out of order. I marvel at the courage of those who do it, but on reflection realize they don't know their danger. I am talking from experience. I have seen the ups and downs of thousands of accounts.

The way to learn to read the tape is to try it. Try it, one stock at a time, with small positions. A very few will have the advantage of knowing someone who understands it. Most of the books and courses (excepting a very few) are theoretical.

One must realize that tape reading and chart reading and all the systems based on using the market's own current action as a forecast of its future are today pretty widespread. I mean by that, practically everyone has a smattering knowledge of them. Of course, what everyone knows isn't worth knowing.

The appearance of each transaction on the tape adds, as it properly should, its mite to determining the market price. One person sees a transaction and thinks it's put there for a reason, so he ignores it or does the opposite of what he feels its appearance is intended to suggest. Another perhaps also thinks he recognizes its character, but feels, coming as it did, that the "sponsorship" is strong and worth following in its current stages anyway. And a third never heard of a transaction occurring for any reason except that someone wanted to buy or sell. He draws still another conclusion. How different is the result than in other lines where things are concealed instead of being brought out into the open.

In any event, the first thing to learn about tape reading is the ability to see the difference between indications recorded on good buying or selling and those which are the result of light-waisted action. This is not any easy thing to do, but is nevertheless essential. Anything one does on the tape is revealing to one who can read it. In the old days, so-called "manipulation," that is, trying to make buyers and sellers react in a common way, was revealing. The good manipulator knew that the very impression he painted on the tape to draw some buying power would generate a certain amount of selling from those who could really understand what they saw.

There are times when one will see "poor buying." But if it is just the start, one might want to follow right along as it sometimes takes months to fill all the outside buy orders once the public gets the bit in its teeth. On the other hand, at the point where every last elevator boy is in stocks, then additional desultory "poor buying" would be a bad thing to follow indeed.

My main point is to develop a realistic attitude; 99.99% and more of those who try to deal in Wall Street think they are right and the tape is wrong. But it's the tape that is watched by both the margin clerk and the tax collector. Stocks that are high and going higher are a good buy. Stocks that are "cheap" and growing cheaper don't interest me from a buying angle.

Statistics, mentioned above, are useful at times and have their place. Sometimes stocks are deadlocked. Statistics are useful in helping to suggest (along with other things) which way they may break out of that sidewise zone. However, I class the tape first and indispensable, and, second, accurate information from brokers and banks on the kinds and amount of buyers, sellers, loans, etc. Then come statistics and all the rest.

1929 Experiences

BACK IN 1929 I had the "privilege" of seeing a very extensive report on a listed corporation. I think it was reputed to have cost $10,000. It was bound in leather. The people who had this compiled bought a lot of the stock analyzed and lost a fortune doing it. Why? Because they stressed individual statistics instead of the tape and because they made several other common mistakes such as forgetting the importance of correct "timing."

At a time like 1929 no real tape reader would have committed an error like this. I actually bought a client 10,000 Radio at 110 as I recall it. I thought it was going straight up. It didn't and we were out at 109.

I saw the top in 1929 and sold stocks in time. It came about, as well as I can recall, something like this: All stocks, of course, did not reach their best prices simultaneously. The issues we traded in not only changed during the year but also narrowed in number. Thus, as this stock and that began to "act" badly, I was switching into those that still acted well. This of itself would eventually result in getting us out altogether. But there were other signs. Ordinary statistics were of no use. Steel common looked cheap enough above 250 on earnings of above $25 a share.

The vogue those days was investment trusts. One house had a special reputation along that line. I forget, but I think it was their third issue. If any new issue (or old one for that matter) should have been a success, that was it. But shortly after the offering it was supported by a "syndicate bid." Well, if ever there was a sign of a market that was overbought here it was. If people couldn't or wouldn't buy that, what could or would they buy? Of course, that wasn't all. There were brokers trying to keep clients from buying more stocks because they couldn't finance them. It was things like this, that told the top of the market. And after the top, the tape told the tale of 1930 and 1931 when the oracles were saying all the way down that everything was OK again.

"Better Late _____ "

THERE IS NO rule about anything in the stock market save perhaps one. That rule is that the key to market tops and bottoms or the key to market advances or declines will never work more than once. The lock, so to speak, is always changed. Therefore, a little horse sense is far more useful than a lot of theory.

However, in a broad way the averages work in favor of those that assume the trend in being will continue until proven changed. This applies both for the company in question, industrially speaking, and price trend of a stock, tape-wise.

"Never argue with the tape" is one saying worth thinking about.

In order for the trend in being to change direction there has to be a change in the influences that caused the trend in the first place. Those that can detect this change before it occurs and becomes generally evident are gifted with powers of analysis and foresight of the very highest order. For most of us detecting the change after it has occurred but before it has proceeded too far is still a very profitable and to many an attainable goal. I think on the average it is better for most of us to be **late and sure** than to be early and doubtful. Many, who thought that various levels on the way down after 1929 to 1932 were buying or turning points, lost the most. The late buyer who came in after 1933 and up quite a bit from the bottom, did quite all right.

Technical Observations

HE **first** new highs for the year after a weak spell usually mean a lot. After scores of shares have been making new highs, the addition of new ones is meaningless.

Volume of trading is also an important factor. It is difficult to define in positive terms. If you are driving a car you can get to your destination more quickly at 50 m.p.h. than at 10 m.p.h. But you may wreck the car at 100 m.p.h. In a similar way increasing volume on an advance up to a point is bullish and decreasing volume on a rally is bearish, but in both cases only up to a point. There are a great many varying circumstances. Experience is the best teacher. Observe the variation in volume, and in time you will learn what it indicates.

GARFIELD
A. DREW

Columbus of the Odd-Lot Theory

One of the most widely accepted technical methods of measuring stock market sentiment is the Odd Lot Index. It was not always so. The man chiefly responsible for their popularization, refinement and interpretation, the Christopher Columbus of the Odd Lot Theory, is Garfield Albee Drew.

Drew was born October 8, 1903, to an old New England family, in Dedham, Massachusetts. He went to Wall Street after graduation from Harvard in 1926, sat out the 1929 crash and early years of depression as a bond statistician. He was later employed by Babson's United Business Service in Boston, and during this period "discovered" odd lots.

In 1940 he published his first treatise on odd lot research and received so many letters from interested investors that he expanded his research into a book. The reception to the book was so gratifying that he set up his own investment service in 1949 with the odd lot concept as its base. He keeps an office in Boston but does most of his work at his home in Newton Center, Massachusetts.

On his choice for a location he said: "What's the point of being in Wall Street? Out here you're aloof from the scuttlebutt, the emotions and social entanglements of life in a financial district." He spends most of his time in sport clothes.

Time magazine called him "The Small Investor's Boswell," and his market philosophy has been widely quoted on the nation's financial pages.

Drew wrote *New Methods for Profits in the Stock Market* in 1941, for Metcalf Press in Boston. Revised editions have been issued since. Most of the passages here from Drew lore are to be found in this volume.

The Wisdom of
GARFIELD A. DREW

The Odd Lotters

(FROM "NEW METHODS FOR STOCK MARKET PROFIT," 1941)

THE TRADING PUBLIC is ordinarily most interested in **this** day, **this** week, and **this** month. It is far more concerned with market movements than with intrinsic values. Business prospects, earnings, and dividends mean little in comparison with a ten point rally or decline, and it is in its largely futile attempts to "catch" these moves perfectly that the public is "wrong."

To go back, a second and more important factor usually missed on odd lot trading is that—because it is essentially a speculative "quick-turn" affair—its volume is always directly proportional to the total volume of trading. Therefore, it is not the number of shares bought or sold on balance that is important, but the proportions of buying or selling to each other.

Most important, however, is the fact that **THE TREND OF SENTIMENT AS INDICATED BY THE ODD LOT BALANCE OF TRADING IS MORE IMPORTANT THAN THE SIDE ON WHICH THE BALANCE LIES.**

Both of the comments quoted above drew their conclusions from whether a buying or selling balance actually existed prior to any given market movement, and disregarded entirely the significance of changes in the size of either balance. To illustrate, odd lot trading will be well on the buying side at the bottom of a drastic decline, but it will be proportionately less so than it was on the way down. The weekly balances never show a preponderance of selling around important bottoms, although on a few individual days there may be such a balance. Primarily, it is always just a matter of less buying. The converse is true with respect to odd lot selling on a top, although here there will be more times when an actual buying balance exists.

These conclusions were derived from a statistical usage of the daily odd lot purchases and sales (available continuously since March, 1936) which will be described later. However, they are also borne out by the monthly data employed by the Brookings Institution which found that on the more important trends the odd lot public invariably bought on declines. Its action on advances was about equally divided between buying and selling.

Thus, although the public is never "wrong" in the sense that it buys around every bottom, it is almost invariably wrong in that it buys proportionately less at the bottom than it did on the way down. Similarly, as an advance progresses toward its peak, selling may either become less or change to actual buying. A change of sentiment on the part of the public after any market trend has become well established is almost always just the opposite of what it should be.

On Stocks and Cash

T HE AVERAGE INVESTOR likes to keep his money "working" for as large a return as possible, and ordinarily abhors what he feels is the futility of holding cash or the equivalent (such as high-grade, short-term bonds). What he fails to realize is that, in a period of declining stock prices, cash which is allocated to common stocks is actually an appreciating asset. If an investor sells a stock at 100, holds the proceeds of the sale until the price reaches 50, and then reinvests in the same issue, his money has doubled in terms of that stock since he can buy with the same amount of dollars twice as many shares as he sold.

The "Industry Group" Approach

I T HAS BEEN pointed out that if the right industries could be selected, it would be possible always to be invested in common stocks which were in a rising price trend. Even in the devastating bear market of 1929-1932, gold stocks were an exception to the rule of declining prices. All other things being equal, a business depression benefits gold producers because the full production can be sold at a fixed price, while costs go down. Thus, the investor would have enjoyed a constantly increasing value who had bought steels in 1915, switched into merchandising stocks in 1918, oils in 1919, rails in 1920, utilities in 1922, electrical equipments in 1926, gold shares in 1929, liquor shares in 1932, silver shares in 1933, automobiles in 1935, aircrafts in 1938-39, railroads in 1941, amusements in 1945, oils in 1946, and no doubt **something** in 1948.

Using hindsight, it is easy to see what could have been done in this respect. In practice, it obviously involves putting all investment eggs in one basket. Few would dare to go to this extreme. Secondly, it involves a tremendous amount of one sort of "forecast"—in fact, a far more difficult type of forecast than is ordinarily the case with "timing." To buy gold stocks in 1929, for example, the investor would have had to foresee a long business depression of considerable severity. At the other extreme, he might have sold on the basis of the Dow Theory or some other trend method, content merely to wait until the trend proved to have changed and without any attempt to foresee exactly what might happen.

Growth Stocks

T HE THIRD APPROACH which eliminates timing attempts to solve the problem of confining all purchases to "growth stocks" on the comfortable theory that, whatever happens to them temporarily in declining markets, they will always go ahead to new highs afterward. Growth stocks are the equities of companies whose earnings have demonstrated underlying long-term growth and give indications of continued secular growth in the future.

As a group, chemicals have been the most outstanding example of "growth stocks" within the last two decades. The 1929 investor in Monsanto Chemical at its high (equivalent for the present stock) of $13\frac{1}{2}$, for example, suffered during the next three years when the price dropped to $2\frac{1}{4}$, but he saw it recover to his cost in 1933, reach new highs at 36 and 40 in 1937 and 1940, drop again to 22 in 1942, and hit a new all-time high at 64 in 1946-47. Basically, this reflected a long-term expansion in sales and earnings, due to the exploitation of new discoveries and products by an exceptionally able management. Conversely, the stocks of some older and more mature companies like U.S. Steel, American Telephone, and General Electric have never since come anywhere near their 1929 highs.

There are obvious advantages in the theory of growth stock investment, but there are still many risks in that some unforeseen element may change the growth factor, or so great a premium may be paid for it that the anticipated new highs do not materialize, to say nothing of the fact that a severe business depression and bear market would—temporarily at least—make the picture look extremely sick.

Like Monsanto, the outstanding "growth stocks" of the last twenty years sold at higher prices in 1937 than in 1929 and at higher prices in 1946 than in 1937, but how many could have been initially selected? Few investors had ever heard of Monsanto in 1929, and if they believed in the long-term future of the chemical industry would have been much more likely to have selected duPont. As an individual organization, it was simply farther along the road to maturity at that time.

The point is that "growth stocks" are seldom outstandingly attractive by the time their growth qualities are widely recognized. This may conceivably be true of the chemicals today. The potentialities of the industry have been so widely touted for several years that the investor at present price levels for the stocks of the leading companies is already paying a considerable premium for those potentialities. Stocks of even the most promising companies frequently sell at levels which only the remote future can justify, and at times discount even the future beyond the point of ultimate realization. Price-to-earnings ratios of 20 or 25 for some chemical stocks are, in effect, already discounting a doubling of earnings at the potential peak that may or may not materialize. Even if it does, the stocks would not necessarily be worth then more than they are selling for now, since the attainment of earnings maturity would not justify the same high price-to-earnings ratios that now exist. Hence, to invest most successfully in growth companies, one must recognize them for what they are—or will be—well ahead of the crowd and thus buy only at a reasonable price.

None of the foregoing comments is intended to disparage the "growth stock" approach. It is a more practical solution than the attempt always to be in the exceptional industry group. On the other hand, as a long-term program, it is a difficult one for the individual investor or even the professional analyst because it is likely to require the most intimate and continuous knowledge of companies and managements as well as industry prospects. The individual probably has a better chance with "timing," because the assumption is not justified that growth stock investment is the best answer on the ground that "forecasting" is impossible. Granting that mistakes will inevitably be made in dealing with the price swings, it is certainly questionable whether there is not just as much room for error in attempting to pick growth stocks at the right time and price.

On the Technical Approach

E VEN THE FUNDAMENTALISTS who decry "technical market timing" say that purchases should only be made when the general price level is low and then sold when the level is high "as judged by objective standards"—something that is likely to result in very poor timing indeed. How high is high? Stocks seemed irrationally "high" in 1927 to experienced investors, but during the next two years they went much higher. Similarly, they seemed "low" in 1931, but they soon after sold at one-third of their average price of that year.

There have been frequent occasions when technical analysis was the **only** thing that could possibly have given the correct answer to the future trend of the market. This was true, for example, in the spring of 1946. If any investor had then possessed a crystal ball which would have shown him what corporate earnings were to be a year later, he could only have concluded that stock prices would be considerably higher. Instead, they were substantially lower in the face of record earnings and dividends.

There was nothing in the "fundamentals"—either in 1946 or 1947—to explain why prices had collapsed in the meantime. But there was considerable evidence of a weak **technical** situation in the market beforehand. . . . It did not seem to make sense, but it was there. The investor who acted on technical grounds did not need to concern himself with **why** the market should seem to be acting irrationally, whereas the analyst of business facts and possibilities—unable to find a "reason"—was forced to conclude that the market could not do what it actually did.

On Predicting the Averages

I N EARLY MAY, 1946, a well-known financial editor asked five specialists in railroad securities to tell him where they thought the Dow-Jones Railroad Average —then around 63—would be in three months, six months, and twelve months. The independent answers of all five were surprisingly close for each period of time, but the average level predicted compared as follows with the facts.

	Average Predicted Level	Actual Level
After three months	65.4	62
After six months	83.4	50
After twelve months	106.0	43

Thus, for the prediction covering one year, there was actually a decline of nearly 32% as against an anticipated gain of more than 68%. Now, the point is that the analysts polled were not amateurs carried away by bullish enthusiasm. Their forecasts were based on sober, expert appraisal of what railroad earning power would be, and in this respect, they were entirely correct.

But, to predict a market level involves another type of forecast. It is necessary not only to estimate future earnings correctly, but in addition to form an opinion as to how those earnings will be appraised by future buyers and sellers. In other words, will investment psychology be pessimistic or optimistic? The particular group involved here not unnaturally assumed that railroad stocks would continue to sell in the same relationship to earnings that prevailed at the time they were making their calculations. For that reason only, their forecast of market prices proved to be entirely wrong.

Price Earnings Ratios and Psychology

I
N A BROAD sense, the experience of the past ten years
has very clearly demonstrated that the price-to-
earnings ratio is a much more important factor than
the actual level and/or trend of earnings themselves.
Since the ratio is determined by investment psychology,
the study of technical market action has, on the whole,
been more fruitful than fundamental analysis. As in the
case of the railroad analysts, it was quite possible to be
perfectly correct in estimating future earnings, but entirely wrong on the level of stock prices at the same time.

From 1938 to 1948, earnings and stock prices pursued
different courses. The reasons for the diverse trends are
quite understandable, but it should nevertheless have
been an illuminating experience for the businessman investor accustomed to an orthodox relationship.

Corporate profits were at their lowest ebb in 1938
when the Dow-Jones Industrial Average rose to nearly
160—a level not seen again until 1945. Profits more than
doubled, however, from 1938 through 1941 in reflection
of war and "defense" orders, but because of the war back-

ground, stock prices pursued a downward course. Excess profits taxes and—later—strikes and material shortages brought about a generally declining trend in earnings during the 1942-46 period, but stock prices rose in anticipation of the high postwar profits which actually materialized by 1947. Again conforming to contrary and apparently illogical behavior, however, the stock market dropped in 1946-47 as corporate earnings rose sharply. Investor psychology swung to the view that such earnings were just too good to last.

ROBERT D. EDWARDS   and   JOHN MAGEE

Master Chart Interpreters

Whether investors are individually pro or anti-charts they can probably agree on one point: the best source book and authority on chart interpretation is a work by Edwards and Magee.

Edwards is related to R. W. Schabacker, who was the first man to spell out chart patterns in early Wall Street years.

John Magee, a close friend and disciple of Edwards, is a graduate of Massachusetts Institute of Technology and initially approached the stock market from an engineering point of view.

Specializing in horticulture at Cornell, Robert Edwards worked for a time for W. Atlee Burpee of Philadelphia. When his brother-in-law, R. W. Schabacker, died in the late 1930's, Edwards took over the management of the Schabacker Institute. In 1941 he came to Springfield, Massachusetts, where he worked for 10 years as Senior Technician for the Stock Trend Service, a position which was later filled by John Magee.

With Magee, he went over the work of Schabacker and added to it using the basic material as a foundation for a refined and greatly expanded statement of technical theory, which became "Technical Analysis of Stock Trends," the definitive volume on the subject, which in its successive revisions and re-publications had, by 1964, reached the fourteenth printing of its fourth edition.

On leaving Springfield in 1951, Edwards moved to South Carolina, where he became a teacher of science at the Georgetown High School with which he is still connected.

John Magee has remained in the investment field. He is president of John Magee, Inc., Springfield, Massachusetts, which maintains daily charts of most listed stocks on the New York and American Stock Exchanges. Copies of these are supplied on request to clients, and they form the foundation of a stock advisory service. The organization also publishes books, and produces chart paper and supplies for market technicians.

Magee has written a number of articles for national publications, has lectured and conducted seminars in his subjects, and was a member of the faculty of the Springfield Evening Adult Schools for eight years, teaching a course on "The Semantics of Wall Street."

The Wisdom of
EDWARDS AND MAGEE

An Outline of the Technical Approach

I T IS EASY, in a detailed study of the many and fascinating phenomena which stock charts exhibit, to lose sight of the fact that they are only the rather imperfect instruments by which we hope to gauge the relative strength of supply and demand, which in turn exclusively determines what way, how fast and how far a stock will go.

Remember that in this work it doesn't in the least matter what **creates** the supply and the demand. The fact of their existence and the balance between them are all that count. No man, no organization (and we mean this **verbatim et literatim**) can hope to know and accurately to appraise the infinity of factual data, mass moods, individual necessities, hopes, fears, estimates and guesses which, with the subtle alterations ever proceeding in the general economic framework, combine to generate supply and demand. But the summation of all these factors is reflected virtually instantaneously in the market.

The technical analyst's task then is to interpret the action of the market itself—to read the flux in supply and demand mirrored therein. For this task, charts are the most satisfactory tools thus far devised. Lest you become enrapt, however, with the mechanics of the chart—the minutiae of daily fluctuations—ask yourself constantly, "What does this action really mean in terms of supply and demand?"

Judgment is required, and perspective, and a constant reversion to first principles. A chart, as we have said and should never forget, is not a perfect tool; it is not a robot; it does not give all the answers quickly, easily and positively, in terms that anyone can read and translate at once into certain profit.

We have examined and tested exhaustively many technical theories, systems, indexes and devices which have not been discussed in this book, chiefly because they tend to short-circuit judgment to seek the impossible by a purely mechanical approach to what is very far indeed from a purely mechanical problem. The methods of chart analysis which have been presented herein are those which have proved most useful because they are relatively simple and for the most part, easily rationalized, because they stick closely to first principles; because they are of a nature that does not lead us to expect too much of them; because they supplement each other and work well together.

Let us review these methods briefly. They fall roughly into four categories:

PART I

The area patterns or formations of price fluctuation which, with their concomitant volume, indicate an important change in the supply-demand balance. They can signify consolidation, a recuperation or gathering of strength for renewed drive in the **same direction** as the trend which preceded them. Or they can indicate reversal, the playing out of the forces formerly prevailing and the victory of the opposing force, resulting in a new drive in the **reverse direction.** In either case, they may be described as periods during which energy is brewed or pressure built up to propel prices in a move (up or down) which can be turned to profit. Some of them provide an indication as to how far their pressure will push prices.

These chart formations, together with volume, furnish the technician with most of his "get in" and many of his "get out" signals.

Volume, which has not been discussed in this book as a feature apart from price action and which cannot, in fact, be utilized as a technical guide by itself, deserves some further comment. Remember that it is **relative,** that it tends naturally to run higher near the top of a Bull Market than near the bottom of a Bear Market. Volume "follows the trend"; i.e., it increases on rallies and decreases on reactions in an over-all up trend, and vice-versa. But use this rule judiciously; do not place too much dependence on the showing of a few days, and bear in mind that **even in a Bear Market** (except during panic moves) there is always a slight tendency for activity to pick up on rises. **("Prices can fall of their own weight, but it takes buying to put them up.")**

A notable increase in activity, as compared with previous days or weeks, may signify either the beginning (breakout) or the end (climax) of a move, temporary or final. (More rarely it may signify a "shakeout.") Its meaning in any given case can be determined by its relation to the price pattern.

PART II

Trend and trendline studies, which supplement area patterns as a means of determining the general direction in which prices are moving and of detecting changes in direction. Although lacking in many cases the nice definition of area formations, they may frequently be used for "get in" and "get out" purposes in short-term trading, and they provide a defense against premature relinquishment of profitable long-term positions.

PART III

Support and resistance levels created by the previous trading and investing commitments of others. They may serve to indicate where it should pay to take a position, but their more important technical function is to show where a move is likely to slow down or end, at what level it should encounter a sudden and important increase in supply or demand as the case may be.

Before entering a trade, look both to the pattern of origin for an indication of the power behind the move and to the history of support resistance for an indication as to whether it can proceed without difficulty for a profitable distance. Support resistance studies are especially useful in providing "cash in" or "switch" signals.

PART IV

Broad market background, including the Dow Theory. Do not scorn this time-tested device for designating the (presumed) prevailing Major trend of the market. Its signals are "late" but, with all its faults (and one of these is the greatly augmented following it has acquired in recent years, resulting in a considerable artificial stimulation of activity at certain periods), it is still an invaluable adjunct to the technical trader's kit of tools.

The general characteristics of the various stages in the stock market's great Primary Bull and Bear cycles should never be lost to view. This brings us back to the idea of **perspective** which we emphasized as essential to successful technical analysis at the beginning of our summary. It is true that you cannot buy or sell "the market"; you can deal only in individual stocks. But that stock which does not to some degree follow the Major trend of the market as a whole is an extraordinary exception. More money has been lost by buying perfectly good stocks in the later and most exciting phases of a Bull Market and then selling them, perhaps from necessity in the discouraging conditions prevailing in a Bear Market than from all other causes combined!

So, keep your perspective on the broad market picture. The basic economic tide is one of the most important elements in the supply-demand equation for each individual stock. It may pay to buck "the public" but it does not pay ever to buck the real underlying trend.

Major Bull and Bear Markets have recurred in fairly regular pattern throughout all recorded economic history and there is no reason to suppose that they will not continue to recur for as long as our present system exists. It is well to keep in mind that caution is in order whenever stock prices are at historically high levels, and that purchases will usually work out well eventually when they are at historically low levels.

DR. LEO BARNES

Collector of Profitable Stock Market Ideas

Professor, analyst, editor, and author, Dr. Leo Barnes is one of America's best known contemporary writers on finance and investment. At the time this is published he is Professor and Chairman of the Department of Finance and Investments at The School of Business of Hofstra University, and is also a member of the Editorial Board of *Business Economics,* the journal of the National Association of Business Economists. He has taught and lectured in his chosen field at Johns Hopkins, Brown, Rutgers, the City University of New York and the New School for Social Research, and has also been engaged as a consultant on investments and economics for many large corporations.

Dr. Barnes is widely known as the author and compiler of *Your Investments,* one of the best selling stock market books of the past decade, and also authored *Buying Guide to Mutual Funds and Investment Companies* (five editions 1956-60), *Handbook for Business Forecasting* (1950), and was a contributor to the *Encyclopedia of Stock Market Techniques* (1963), the *Business Finance Handbook* (1953), and is a frequent contributor to the Financial Analyst's Journal. Just prior to his present post at Hofstra University, he was chief economist for Prentice Hall, Inc.

The Wisdom of
DR. LEO BARNES

How to Beat Market Swings by Formula Plans

(FROM "YOUR INVESTMENTS," 1966 EDITION)

F ORMULA PLANS ARE designed in advance for automatic buying and selling action when the predetermined signals are given. In most forms, they compel caution in bull markets and bravery in bear markets. They automatically (even if only partially) achieve the investment target of buying cheap and selling dear. They impel you to sell as prices rise and force you to buy as prices decline.

Formula plans can definitely improve the batting average of most investors. While they deliberately avoid maximum **theoretical** profits, they more than make up for this by substantially cutting potential losses. Only the exceptional investor or speculator can hope to outperform a good formula plan **in the long run.**

Many different formula plans have been introduced, developed, and perfected since 1937. In this chapter, you will find typical examples of more popular and useful formula plans. You will also find some simplifications and modifications of such plans that will make them easier to use. You will probably be able to tailor at least one plan for your own use.

CONSTANT DOLLAR FORMULA PLANS

This is the simplest type of formula plan. It is probably also the least effective. You simply decide in advance how many **dollars** you wish to have invested in stocks. Then, if the market rises, at predetermined time intervals (say quarterly), you sell stocks to reduce your holdings to that dollar value. If the market declines, you buy stocks to raise your holdings to that dollar value. When you sell stocks, you either buy bonds with the proceeds or put the money in a savings account.

This method is obviously easy, but gains are very limited.

CONSTANT RATIO PLANS

In this type of plan, you decide in advance what per cent of your investment funds should be in stocks—say 40%, 50%, 60%, or 70%. Then, at predetermined time intervals, you sell or buy stocks to restore or maintain the predetermined ratio of stocks regardless of the level of stock prices.

EXAMPLE: You start with an investment fund of $15,000. You decide that you should keep 60% of it (or $9,000 to start) in good quality common stocks, and the remaining 40% of it (or $6,000 to start) partly in E bonds and partly in savings and loan accounts. You buy accordingly.

After six months, you find that the stock market has risen, so that the total value of your fund is $2,000 more, or $17,000. Your stocks are now worth $11,000. That is roughly 65% of $17,000. Therefore, you must sell $800 worth of stocks to reduce your holdings to $10,200, or 60% of $17,000. You then put more in savings and loan accounts with the $800 (less commissions and taxes).

You thus have salted away some of your bull market profits, but also have kept some of them invested for a possible further gain. And, because you have bought more fixed income investments, you are not as vulnerable to a decline.

Suppose, however, that your $15,000 investment fund was set up just before the market took a turn for the worse. In six months, instead of rising in value by $2,000 it declines by that amount. Your total fund is now worth only $13,000. Your stocks are now valued at $7,000, 54% of $13,000.

Under your constant ratio formula, you must now buy $800 more of stocks to bring your stockholdings up to $7,800, or 60% of $13,000. You use some of your savings and loan funds to do this.

You do it no matter how scared you are that the market is going to drop some more. When you are following a formula plan, you soon learn to regard falling prices as a chance to buy more stocks at a lower price to help make up paper losses.

WHEN TO ADJUST PORTFOLIOS

How often do you change your portfolio to restore the predecided stock ratio? Obviously, you do not want to do it too often. If you do, you cut your profits short and run up your commissions and taxes excessively. Therefore, in practice, before restoring your stock ratio, you should wait until the value of your total fund has increased or decreased by at least 10%. Many followers of this simple formula approach prefer to wait for a 15% or 20% move.

If you are an inexperienced investor, the constant ratio plan is probably a good jumping-off point for formula-type investing—with part of your funds only. It will work only in a complete market cycle—both down and up. It will work well only if that cycle included some comparatively wide swings. It does not make much money on narrower fluctuations. To take advantage of smaller price shifts, various variable ratio formula plans have been developed.

VARIABLE RATIO PLANS

Under such plans, the percentage of stocks in a fund is stepped up as stock prices decline and lowered as stock prices rise. For example, at bull market peaks, you are only 5-10% in stocks, 90-95% in bonds.

At bear market bottoms you are 90-95% in stocks, only 5-10% in bonds.

This obviously gives better results than the constant ratio plan. You have bought substantially more stock at low prices and sold substantially more stock at high prices. For this reason, it is mathematically certain that a variable ratio plan will do better than either the average investor or the "buy-and-hold-forever" investor—but only as long as the stock market continues to fluctuate around some central average.

There are four main problems you face in setting up a variable ratio formula plan. You can best understand the whole technique if you think about these problems.

1. How to get the central stock price average? Any variable ratio formula plan revolves around the central average or median market price selected. How do you determine it? Do you use historical price ranges? Or do you rely on average price-earnings ratios, average price-dividend ratios, or average stock-bond yield spreads?

2. What stock-bond ratios? What ratios of stocks and bonds (or, more generally, aggressive securities and defensive investments) should be maintained at estimated market highs, market lows, and average market levels? For example, are you 50% in stocks and 50% in bonds at the estimated average? A more conservative ratio? A more speculative ratio?

3. How many price zones? How many different price zones or percentage ratios or steps should you set up? Do you have price zones for every 5% change in ratios, every 10%, or every 20%?

4. How often to buy and sell? When and how often do you buy or sell securities to achieve the indicated ratios? Do you buy or sell as soon as a particular step is reached, or do you wait? Do you have different rules for changing ratios in bull markets and in bear markets?

DETERMINING THE CENTRAL STOCK PRICE AVERAGE

Successful operation of a variable ratio formula plan depends largely on the selection of a properly located average or median zone. If—for example, because of either runaway or creeping inflation—stock market prices zoom far above your selected median and never return, your formula plan will quickly become utterly obsolete. You will be completely in bonds or cash and never permitted to get back into stocks. On the other hand, should your averages zone be placed too high, your formula plan will be operating on a more speculative basis than you originally intended. The first predicament has often happened; the latter, rarely if ever.

Three kinds of answers to this basic problem have been developed over the past 20-plus years.

THE HISTORICAL APPROACH

Here the middle zone is set in terms of stock price patterns of the past, presumably with more attention paid to the recent past. No long-term growth trend in stock prices is assumed. In the depression '30's, before World War II and after the stock market debacle of 1929, such an approach was natural.

What has happened to formula plans using this approach? A dramatic answer is given by the fate of one of the first variable ratio formula plans—that of Vassar College, started in 1938. Under its zoning timetable, the fund was supposed to be completely out of stocks and completely in bonds when the Dow-Jones Industrial average hit the (post 1929) historically high level of 206. That point was reached in 1945 and, in its old form, the fund would not have bought since then.

THE GROWTH OR TREND APPROACH

To overcome the error of the strictly historical approach illustrated above, it is here assumed that the stock market is in a definite long-term upward trend. Therefore, the central zone of a formula plan should be higher each year, in step with the long-term trend.

An example of this approach is the "Seven Step Variable Ratio Plan," several formulations of which have been used by the Keystone Custodian Funds of Boston.

The original plan was based on 1897-1941 experience, which showed stock prices rising an average of 3% per year. When this pace of increase turned out to be inadequate for the bull market of the fifties, a second plan was developed in terms of an average stock price gain of 4.4% per year, based on 1933-1957 experience.

But even this pace of gain was unable to keep up with the bull market of the late fifties and early sixties. So a third formula plan, based on 1946-1957 experience of an average 8.2% gain in stock prices per year, came into force.

Even under this most generous formulation, in late 1964 investors would have been 80-90% in bonds or other defensive holdings, and only 10-20% in common stocks.

THE RATIO OR "CASUAL" APPROACH

The growth approach, like the historical approach it supplanted, is still open to the criticism that it relies too much on historical stock price levels. The fact that stock averages have risen an average of 3% per year—or 8% per year—for many years is no guarantee that they will continue to do so. What's more, in any single year, stocks could rise or fall 25% or more, rather than rise 3% or 8%. Therefore, any plan tied directly to specific price ranges is not fully satisfactory. It cannot achieve maximum year-to-year results.

What is needed is a means of tying a formula plan to the determinants of stock prices, rather than to stock prices themselves. In this way, if the factors determining stock prices change—because of inflation, the growing importance of institutional investment, some basic change in investor psychology, or for any other reason—the formula plan will not be automatically and swiftly outmoded.

This is the essence of the ratio or "casual" approach to formula planning. Here the central price zone is geared not to price levels as such, but to some measure which, it is believed, determines, reflects, or anticipates the level of stock prices.

Favorite measures that have been used for this purpose include latest reported overall dividend yields and price-earnings ratios. Alternatively, price-cash-flow ratios could be employed. Or a strictly economic (rather than financial) measure—like the level of total national product (GNP)—could be utilized.

It is even possible that a formula plan could be geared to some strictly technical yardstick rather than a basic value measure. A single favored technical indicator could be used. It probably would be more fruitful, however, to link a formula plan with some consensus of a number of technical indicators.

To illustrate formula plans based on all these possible variations, and to facilitate your own formula planning, we have drawn up three alternative plans—each geared to overall dividend yields, price-earnings ratios, price-cash-flow ratios, and a consensus of technical indicators—that seem suitable for market conditions in 1966-68.

The difference among the three plans shown on the inside back cover is highlighted by the nature of the portfolios they called for in September 1965, when the Dow-Jones industrial average was about 935, the DJIA price-earnings ratio about 18 to 1, and its price-cash-flow ratio about 10.5 to 1. Under the ultra-conservative plan, you would have been down to 35% in stocks and 65% in bonds, cash, or cash equivalents. Under the conservative plan, your stock-bond ratio would be 50-50. Under the moderately speculative plan, you would have been 65% in stocks, 35% in bonds, cash, or equivalents.

Other, more complicated standards have also been developed for formula plans based on the ratio or casual approach. Perhaps the one which has achieved the greatest public interest is that of Graham, Dodd, and Cottle in their *Security Analysis* (fourth edition, 1962).

The authors work out a central annual value for the Dow-Jones industrials in terms of average earnings of the 30 D-J stocks for the previous 10 years, capitalized on a basis equivalent to 1.33 times the recent yield of top-grade bonds. In earlier editions, Mr. Graham had called for capitalizing stocks at twice the yield of high-grade bonds.

Even with the current more generous capitalization for stocks, fair price levels under the formula were far below actual stock prices near the end of 1965, and would have called for the sale of all common stock holdings. Indeed, the formula would have missed the entire 1961-65 bull market.

CONSERVATIVE OR SPECULATIVE STOCK-BOND RATIOS

Ratios can be varied all the way from 100% stocks at estimated bear market lows to 100% bonds at estimated bull market highs. For any plan, you have to work out a range table similar to those exemplified in the plans on the inside back cover, indicating the ratios of defensive and aggressive investments in your portfolios in the seven zones.

A crucial test of your conservative or speculative approach occurs at the estimated average or median price range or bracket, around which you assume stock market prices will fluctuate. In such a median bracket, the ultraconservative investor may decide to be 65% in bonds and 35% in stocks. The moderately conservative investor may decide to be 50% in both bonds and stocks. A more speculative investor may choose to be only 35% in defensive securities and 65% in common stocks at the center point.

It is instructive, however, to note the conclusions of a careful study of variable ratio formula plans made by the First National Bank of Birmingham, Alabama, under the direction of Mr. Charles F. Zukoski, Jr. The study examined the relative results over the 25-year period from 1924 to 1950 with different stock-bond ratios at the median range. This span of years covers both the incredible speculative boom of 1929 and the equally incredible bust of 1932-33.

Conclusion of the study: The larger the per cent of common stocks required by the formula at the median range, the greater the capital appreciation and income received over the whole 25-year period. What's more, within the 25 years, funds using higher stock ratios did not fall in value below those using lower stock ratios—even in the depression years of 1932-33 or in the sharp market breaks of 1937 and 1942.

HOW TO IMPROVE FORMULA PLAN RESULTS

The very essence of formula plans is to sell out most stocks well before bull market peaks and buy most stocks well before bear market bottoms.

This bothers many investment managers. They would like to sell more stocks in the higher zones 6 and 7, near bull market peaks; and buy more stocks in zones 1 and 2, near bear market bottoms. Undoubtedly this would improve results for the formula over a complete bull and bear market cycle.

Since you are supposed to be operating under an automatic formula, however, you cannot be asked to use your judgment to decide whether a bull market or bear market trend will continue. But there are some supplementary rules and techniques for riding the trend a little longer:

1. Wait a month or two before buying or selling. Do not act on the very first day called for by your formula. Wait to confirm the trend. This is probably a good formula rule—if the exact waiting period is specified and not left to the investor's judgment, and if it is not too long.

2. Act at the mid-point of the zone, not at the top or bottom. This is another delaying tactic. Actually, all it does is to shift the action points called for by a formula up or down.

3. Use stop-loss orders. When your formula stock selling point is reached in a rising market, put in a stop order to sell a few points below the current market level. Then, if the up-trend continues, you have not sold stocks too soon.

In the opposite direction, when your formula stock buying point is reached in a declining market, you put in a stop order to buy a few points above the current market. Then, if the down-trend continues, you have not bought stocks too soon.

In practice, this device can become a virtual abandonment of the variable ratio formula plan—unless the stop-loss point is placed very close to the current market level. Indeed, an entirely different "technical" technique, based on the continuous use of stop orders, has been developed.

4. Change stock-bond ratios if necessary. Suppose you find that your formula plan is out of step with the actualities of current stock prices, earnings and dividends—that, as has been the case for many earlier formula plans, you have been too conservative. How and when do you change your stock-bond ratios? To change your zoning plan at or near the top of a bull market is not very effective. The reason is that you are largely out of stocks anyhow. To invest very heavily in stocks at such a high level of the market is risky.

It is much more effective to make a zoning change when the market drops into the middle or lower zones of your plan. At that time you will be more substantially invested in stocks, which will then appreciate in the subsequent market rise.

HOW TO SELECT SECURITIES FOR FORMULA PLANS

Formula plans are essentially timing formulas, not formulas for selecting stocks and bonds. They are formulas for when, not for what. Yet the purpose of formula plans is to minimize the need and occasion for both judgment and emotionally influenced decisions. Therefore, the securities you plan to buy and sell under a formula plan should as far as possible be designated—or at least described or defined—in advance.

HOW TO SELECT STOCKS TO BUY OR SELL

In theory, it is possible for a formula plan to use almost any one of many techniques for selecting securities. You can use either the fundamental or technical approach, buy only market leaders or only market laggards, only growth stocks or only income stocks, and so on. Whatever method of selection you use, it is usually wise to concentrate on a specific eligible list of securities from which buying selections will be made.

Some larger formula plans buy all the 65 stocks in the Dow-Jones composite average. Others concentrate on a dozen or so leading blue chips only. Still others choose from among "The Favorite Fifty" of the experts. Still others choose from among even larger diversified lists, such as the 100 top institutional favorites.

Some formula funds make a practice of buying volatile, high-leverage stocks in the lower buying zones but less volatile ones in the higher buying zones. Correspondingly, they sell the more volatile ones first in zones above the median. This practice will increase capital gain over the entire cycle.

If you are attracted by the formula approach but have not too much time for security selection, consider investing in several representative closed-end investment companies or similarly diversified mutual funds.